chasing joy

The writings of Ed Hays have had a definite impact on my spiritual journey. His creative, refreshing style is always joined with depth and wisdom. Ed Hays' books have helped me find innovative ways to pray holistically and to live in a meaningful, joy-filled manner.

Joyce Rupp
Best-selling author of *May I Have This Dance?* and
co-author of *The Circle of Life*

Edward Hays has been a pioneer manifesting a daring mystical sensibility and an unbridled imagination that makes his vision of Christianity consistently fresh and invigorating. All of his books are graced with an appreciation for all the world's religions, popular culture, and humor.

Frederic and Mary Ann Brussat
SpiritualityandPractice.com

Fr. Ed Hays is in the vanguard of spiritual writers who remind us over and over that God is in our lives, in the midst of our messy world, that Christianity is about incarnation. The task of twenty-first century saints, Ed Hays reminds us, will be to find God in the ten thousand things of the here and now.

Rich Heffern
Senior writer for the *National Catholic Reporter* and
author of *Daybreak Within: Living in a Sacred World*

There are few people who consistently give us both depth and breadth—while never closing that clever and humorous edge— as does Ed Hays. If a holy man is one who does not take himself too seriously, then Ed is such a man. Fortunately, he always takes God and his readers very seriously!

Richard Rohr, O.F.M.
Center for Action and Contemplation
Albuquerque, New Mexico

chasing joy

musings on life in a bittersweet world

edward hays
author of *Prayers for the Domestic Church*

Forest of Peace  Notre Dame, IN

Unless otherwise noted, the author has provided his own scripture translations.

Founded in 1865, Ave Maria Press is a ministry of the Indiana Province of Holy Cross.

www.forestofpeace.com

ISBN-10 0-939516-78-0   ISBN-13 978-0-939516-78-0

Cover art © Neil Brennan/Veer

Cover and text design by Katherine Robinson Coleman

Printed and bound in the United States of America.

Library of Congress Cataloging-in-Publication Data

    Hays, Edward M.
     Chasing joy : musings on life in a bittersweet world / Edward Hays.
       p. cm.
     ISBN-13: 978-0-939516-78-0 (pbk.)
     ISBN-10: 0-939516-78-0 (pbk.)
     1. Joy—Religious aspects—Christianity. 2. Happiness—Religious aspects—Christianity. 3. Christian life. I. Title.
     BV4647.J68H39 2007
     242—dc22

                       2006033716

Contents

Be always **Joyful**,
Pray continually,
and **give Thanks** in all circumstances,
for this is the will of God for you.

1 Thessalonians 5:16–18

This book, titled *Chasing Joy*, is but another expression of the pursuit of happiness as one of our God-given inalienable rights that Thomas Jefferson included in the Declaration of Independence. The quest of happiness isn't an easy one in today's bittersweet world as we are nourished daily on media meals of cheerless stories of war and the horrors of torture, murder, and street violence. Not only must we face all this bad news, but we must also deal with our own personal difficulties and disappointments. Everyday life certainly challenges those of us who sincerely desire to live the Good News proclaimed by the angels at Bethlehem and expressed in that exultant old Christmas carol, "Joy to the world, the Lord is come!"

In his first letter to the Thessalonians, written only twenty-five years or so after the death of Jesus, itinerant preacher Paul of Tarsus exhorts his Christian converts of Thessalonica to "rejoice always."[1] His call to live joyously isn't exclusively a Christian one since it is also found in the world's other great religious traditions. Yet to rejoice and strive to live joyously while witnessing the horrifying events of our world seems to be either insane or satanic!

Authors write books for a variety of reasons. I wrote this one because I was inspired during the years I spent writing what is perhaps my favorite book, *The Passionate Troubadour*. It is a medieval novel about Francis of Assisi, renowned for his expansive love of all creation and his radical poverty. For me personally, what makes Francis stand out from the thousands of other saints is not that he was a barefoot, self-impoverished saint, but that he was a merry saint.

His unquenchable joy was long a mystery to me since his life was anything but happy once God had touched him. The Spirit of God inspired his dream of a community of laymen dedicated to simple living and service to those in need, but the Church seriously crippled his vibrant dream by institutionalizing it. To make matters worse, his own Franciscan companions watered down his simple rule, claiming it impossible to live even if Francis himself lived it! Yet to these and other painful disappointments, Francis responded with joyful acceptance, as he also did to the physical afflictions caused by his personal asceticism—the blindness of his later years and the constant pain of his stigmata.

St. Paul said that to "rejoice always" was God's will for us, but he didn't say how to accomplish this seemingly impossible feat. It was clear to me that Francis of Assisi found that ability. As I wrote of his infallible joyfulness, I was inspired to seek the same source of profound joy that Francis had discovered.

However, being inspired to live joyfully in the world in which I live was to be challenged to the extreme. How could I as an American rejoice constantly when my government waged what my conscience said was an immoral war of imperial aggression? How could I rejoice when politicians slashed social programs for the poor and elderly as they simultaneously reduced the taxes on the country's wealthiest? And instead of my church being a source of hope, it too became a cause of sadness as it returned to yesteryear's rituals and legalistic rigidity. How could I be joyful when my church was more concerned with preserving its own image and status than inclusively incorporating the marginal and alienated or working for justice and peace? In my personal life, when my own family or friends were diagnosed with cancer or suffered some tragic catastrophe, how could I respond with joyful acceptance?

The formula "If it bleeds, it leads" is the programming agenda for what news stories lead off a broadcast of our 24/7 news. That outlook and the restless discontent created by unsatisfied desires, coupled with all the disappointments, heartache, and sorrow in our personal lives, make it a real challenge to live a joyful life. It is this very challenge that the following reflections explore as they propose that not only is it possible to live a

joyous life, but one of an unshakable joy that is powerful enough to withstand even the darkest tribulations of
life. Paul wrote that we are to pray always, be grateful in
all circumstances, and always rejoice since it is the will
of God for us. If these three imperatives are indeed the
will of God, then blessedly wise are those who strive
earnestly to live in such unflinching joy! At the Last
Supper, the Teacher bequeathed his invincible, theft-
proof joy to his disciples and then promised, "no one
will take your joy from you."[2] To achieve this unflinching joy, simply use the gift that you have been given.

This book on joyful living is the result of the head-
on collision between my own attempts to imitate a joyful saint of thirteenth-century medieval Italy and the
painful realities of living in today's bittersweet world at
the beginning of the twenty-first century. Perhaps it can
serve you as a survival manual for how to live happily.

EDWARD HAYS
Summer 2006

[1] 1 Thessalonians 5:16
[2] John 16:22

the **impossible** imperative

Rejoicing always is an imperative virtue, one so essential that without living it one is seriously crippled. In his letter to the small convert community of Christians of Thessalonica, Paul told them they were to practice not one but three imperative virtues! Not only were they to rejoice always, but they also were to pray ceaselessly and give thanks—regardless of whatever happened—since these were God's will. These three imperatives present a serious challenge because they are God's will for us. They are indeed divine imperatives. Since any one of them (let alone all three) seems impossible, Paul followed immediately with the admonition, "Do not quench the Spirit."[1]

A multitude of books have been written on the practice of prayer and on living constantly grateful.

However, manuals on how to be authentically joyful, especially in all circumstances and at all times, are not that plentiful. I've intentionally prefaced the word *joy* with *authentic*, since joy or happiness—like other emotions such as sorrow—can be easily counterfeited. For example, in ancient Rome, professional mourners were hired to weep and wail loudly at funerals. While I don't know of any professional rejoicers who can be hired to make weddings more festive, there are those who feel obliged to always appear joyful. This sense of duty arises from their belief that being redeemed in baptism obliges them to be joyful. They attempt to apply the joy of a synthetic cheerfulness like morning makeup —believing that their mirthful mask witnesses to the unbounded joy of being redeemed. Sadly, these artificial smiling faces, being manufactured mirth, are easily recognized as a Christian charade.

There are others who are seemingly always happy: the simple-minded, who once were called "God's Children." Because of their disabled mental capacities, they are able to live joyfully carefree. Theirs is an authentic joy unlike the sometimes pretended joy of the pious, but it is not this kind of joy either that we are challenged to abide in constantly.

To these two groups is added a third who outwardly appear to be always happy and pleasant. These are people who always think positive thoughts about themselves, others, the world, and life. Their religious belief denies the existence of evil and sin! They make a spiritual practice of ignoring the viciousness of poverty, the evils of exploitation, and the host of other horrors that humans daily inflict upon one another. The three imperatives of their happy, pleasant state of life are to 1) think only positive thoughts, 2) practice meditation and other spiritual disciplines, and 3) follow a healthy, wholesome diet and lifestyle. Such spiritual disciplines may create happiness, but living a joyful life doesn't mean always feeling happy and free from tribulations, or even of pain. It likewise doesn't mean living in some dawn-to-dusk ecstasy of perpetual bliss. To be serenely happy (the meaning of *bliss*) is impossible if you are experiencing a migraine headache, undergoing chemotherapy treatments, or lacking food and a roof over your head. *Joy* also doesn't mean the merriment of a wedding dance, a birthday party, or a Mardi Gras parade, since life isn't an endless party. *Joy* and *happiness* are often interchangeable terms, but *happiness* is usually associated with good luck or fortune. As an expression of amusement or entertainment, it understandably cannot be enduring.

The folk expression *happy-go-lucky* describes those who live carefree, untroubled lives. It describes those who are perennially cheerful since they tend to be irresponsible and unconcerned about the practical needs of tomorrow. The Master instructed his disciples to trust in God's providential care. Realistically, he didn't expect his disciples to be happy-go-lucky and unconcerned about their own, or their family's, material needs. His desire was that they should not live in anxiety, fretfully fearful about their physical needs. *Happy-go-lucky* then isn't a spiritual virtue or the same thing as striving to always live a joyful life.

The word *joy* contains feelings of the highest pleasure, delight, happiness, gladness, conviviality, and joviality. This last quality, *joviality*, contains an insight into how to always rejoice. *Jovial* means being full of merriment, that outward cheerfulness that attracts friends and comrades. However, *jovial* also implies a semi-divine state. Originally, it referred to those born under the influence of the planet Jupiter, considered by the ancients to be the source of human happiness. Jupiter was the supreme god of the Romans and was also known as Jove.

To be always jovial does not require being born under the influence of some far-flung planet in the night sky, but rather being reborn as a son or daughter of the Divine Parent, the source of all happiness. Essential to the Spiritual Master of Galilee was that his disciples realize the necessity of being reborn in God's spirit of eternal life and joy. A lifestyle of always rejoicing requires a living consciousness of your divine birthright as a beloved daughter or son of Joy Divine. If you believe you are a beloved child of God, that belief should impact how you experience life that is always bittersweet. When God is consistently experienced as a continuously solicitous, unconditionally loving father or mother, you can respond with trust, even joy, to whatever misfortunes life leaves on your doorstep.

[1] 1 Thessalonians 5:19

invincible joy

Lingering like an echoing mantra is the Master's promise, ". . . and no one will take your joy from you."[1] This ability of the Master's joy to be unconquerable, regardless of whether the odds are overwhelmingly against being victorious, reminds me of the famous Three Musketeers of Alexandre Dumas. The musketeers were a seventeenth-century mounted guard of French gentlemen whose allegiance was exclusively to the service of the king of France. The names of these three famous heroes of Dumas' novels, and later of Hollywood movies, were Athos, Porthos, and Aramis. They never lost a fight or were outwitted by their enemies in a conflict. What made these three so invincible was their fidelity to one another as expressed in their motto, "All for one, and one for all!"

Joy is likewise invincible whenever it acts "All for one, and one for all," side by side with "Pray always, and be always grateful," as did the three musketeers Athos, Porthos, and Aramis. Joy will be defeated easily whenever it tries to act like a lone-ranger virtue when outnumbered by a horde of misfortunes and miseries. Those famous Pauline three—joy, gratitude, and prayer—are identical triplets that sustain, protect, and encourage one another when they are lived side by side.

Always being grateful regardless of the circumstances requires a gift-giver to whom you express thanks. Continuous gratitude is simultaneously prayer to the endlessly generous gift-giver: God. Praying incessantly isn't perpetual recitation of prayers; it is simply abiding in the presence of the Beloved in every place and time. Being conscious of this holy habitat in which you live, breathe, and act will naturally express itself by viewing everything as gift, and this giftedness will burst out as loving thanksgiving. To receive gifts, especially unexpected gifts, is always a most joyous experience. Being awakened to daily life, as an endless avalanche of undeserved gifts, is to find to your delight that you are living a joyous life.

The next reflections will consider ways to respond when life seems to overflow not with gifts but with curses of cancer, other sicknesses, and misfortunes. However, strive today—to the best of your ability—to let the three mystical musketeers of joy, gratitude, and prayer defend your tranquility and happiness.

[1] John 16:22

three

the **glad** game

To rejoice is the natural human response to success, receiving good news, or falling in love. Rejoicing comes easily at these times and at weddings, victory celebrations, and those special holidays of Christmas, Easter, and New Year's Eve. But how can you be joyous when you're sick with the flu, your job has been terminated, or your physician informs you that you have cancer? Only a simple-minded person—not able to grasp the painful or even deadly implications of such news—could rejoice at times like these. Or take the case of just a dreary, boring, gray, overcast day. Is it possible to be cheerful when you are engulfed in lifeless routine?

The challenge is to experiment, to explore the various ways of living in joy when next you find yourself in situations that are not naturally happy. One way is to find creative ways to make the common more colorful or to invent ways to change the dull into the delightful. Another would be by striving not to complain, or if you tend to be crabby and short-tempered, by striving to become long-tempered. Every grace is an art. Becoming long-tempered requires practicing the art of being patient with life's irritating daily issues. This is more than tolerance. It is graceful joy laced with patient waiting based on a personal conviction that out of difficulties, unexpected good can and usually will appear. Any art—playing the piano and being long-tempered in difficult situations—requires repetitive practice and patience.

Consider another irritation: that of the noisy behavior of others such as young teenagers racing their motorbikes up and down your street or celebrating together in front of your house late at night. These and similar actions are logical robbers of your peace and joy that would normally result in anger. Experiment with reverse evolution. Desire to be as young as those noisy teenagers are by shrinking the age difference between you and them in order to share in their uninhibited adolescent joy.

Another way to find joy in difficult circumstances is by use of comparison when forced to endure some misfortune. Retrieve from your past a similar but more painful experience, then place it side by side with your present predicament, and usually a measure of gladness can be mined out of the present difficulty. This type of grateful gladness is contained in the expression, "There but for the grace of God go I," which matches your present state with another's truly painful misfortune.

These are three examples of alternative ways to live happily. Allow them to inspire you to explore your own alternate ways of dealing with unpleasant, difficult situations that seem to make it impossible to be joyful. Remember that despite the various spiritual techniques you employ, you may not be successful—at least not with your first attempts. Also remember that being encouraged to always be joyful isn't an invitation to become a Pollyanna.

In 1913 Eleanor Porter wrote her novel *Pollyanna* about a young girl named Pollyanna Whittier who was constantly playing the smiling "glad game." Pollyanna went to impossible lengths to find something good even in the darkest and most horrible situations. While this trait could be seen as admirable—as a way of rejoicing always and in all circumstances—it wasn't, since her joy was artificial. As a result, her name, Pollyanna, has become a term of ridicule that is used to describe a foolishly cheerful and optimistic man or woman.

Miss Pollyanna wasn't honest, and so what appeared as a positive virtue was flawed because she blinded herself to whatever was unpleasant in life. If you are not self-blinded to reality by living a sheltered life of privilege, then you know there is much that is not only unpleasant in life but also repulsively horrible! To be authentically happy, not full of Pollyanna, make-believe cheerfulness, is the will of God for us. To paraphrase the Lord's Prayer, "Your will—of joyful living—be done, on earth as it is in heaven."

authentic joy

An authentic religious path or spirituality can never be a fire escape from the ghastly evils of humanity or some insulated spiritual cocoon from the repulsive and hideous pains that saturate our world. To be genuinely joyful demands a companionship with the pains and sadness of life, and perhaps the deep wounds of betrayal. Joy must also know the seemingly bottomless dark pit of anguish, enduring the desolation of being imprisoned by one's fears, or the poignant anguish of seething, violent anger. This seemingly impossible pairing of happiness and suffering appears at first to be contradictory, for how can you be joyful in the midst of misery?

Rejoicing when something good happens to you or upon completing a significant work is instinctively spontaneous. What is not instinctive is being joyful when you're suffering the searing pain of amputation in a divorce, the heart-shattering desolation of the death of a child, spouse, or parent, or while enduring intense pain. However, to live a joyful life is not a merely human achievement, and it is not a superhuman one either. Rather, it requires being divinely human—being faithful to your birthing blueprint in which you were designed to be God-like.

Immediately following his three famous imperatives of endless prayer, continuous gratitude, and constant joy, Paul—the wandering minstrel of the Good News— says, "Do not quench the Spirit." He could have reworded it by saying, "Have faith in the Spirit, remember the words of the angel to Mary of Nazareth, 'with God all things are possible.' So don't allow logic to douse the voice of the Spirit Architect Master Builder of your birthing blueprint!"

In his poem "Tintern Abbey," William Wordsworth wrote of the Spirit's work of enkindling joy,

> And I have felt
> A presence that disturbs me with the joy
> Of elevated thoughts; a sense sublime
> Of something far more deeply interfused,
> Whose dwelling is the light of setting suns,
> And the round ocean and the living air,
> And the blue sky, and in the mind of man;
> A motion and a spirit, that impels
> All thinking things, all objects of all thought,
> And rolls through all things.

As we honestly face the harsh realities of life, that "presence" that Wordsworth said disturbed him with joy could also be expressed as:

That sense sublimely divine
so deeply interfused with the pains of childbirth,
the agonies of defeat and failure
Its tabernacle dwelling is in fading light
of the setting suns of dying institutions,
ways of life and loves.
This gnawing sublime spirit impels
all honestly thinking persons
to question the existence of God
as it rolls on and on incessantly
through all our earthen miseries.

A disturbing, jarring joy is felt whenever we experience "The Presence" that confronts us everywhere in life instead of only in sacred places and rituals as we have been piously trained. Perception is at the heart of recognizing the face of God in our miseries as St. Augustine said, "God is always present to us and to all things; it is that we, like blind persons, do not have eyes to see God!"

Such God-seeing eyes seem given only to mystics and poets who are able to find the divine in both the awesomely beautiful and the drably common, as did Elizabeth Barrett Browning, who wrote, "Earth's crammed with heaven, and every common bush alive with God." We thrill at her poetic insight and have on rare occasions in life caught glimpses of this drab Earth crammed with heaven: some spellbinding moment in nature in profound expressions of human love, like sexual union; or in some great work of art. But, Ms. Browning, sometimes to our non-poetic eyes, Earth is "crammed with hell!"

Looking through our television window of today's 24/7 news coverage, we see the ghastly sexual exploitation of children, the genocide of entire peoples, the wanton destruction and death of exploitative wars, vicious tribal conflicts, and bloody terrorist attacks. While piously maintaining that God abides in all places, religion often makes a razor-sharp conceptual division between those places where God is and isn't present. God, the essence of goodness, is clearly present in those places and actions judged good and wholesome. But in those viciously evil, if not diabolical, human actions and circumstances, religion remains silent or attributes them to the Evil One. If St. Augustine and mystical writers can be believed when they claim that God is "always present" in all things, then how can we restrict the Divine Presence to only the good and beautiful? To be able to rejoice always requires an entirely new and radical understanding of the Divine Mystery.

five

holy, holy,
holy is earth
crammed with hell

If yours is the common belief in God, then searching for the presence of the All Holy One in the ugly conflict-ravished miseries of the world is like looking for a needle in a haystack! Time-honored is that belief in a God who, being all good, is the luminous source of blessings and love, while Satan, who is darkness, is the source of all evil and hate. The creed of conventional religion believes in a divided creation with God dwelling in heaven while the devil's domain is this world.

The God of our belief is the God that we encounter. So to find God in the darkness and evils of life requires a belief or an understanding of God as the

Divine Mystery. To believe in the Creator as the sacred, if not supremely ultimate, Mystery requires embracing an enigma, a puzzle that defies our limited human comprehension. Sacred mysteries cannot be explained. Since they can only be embraced, we are challenged to accept an outwardly impossible mystery: God has chosen to be present in what we judge as evil!

God has entered into intimate communion with the agonies of our pain and suffering, the misery of human cruelty to one another and to animals, and in the butchery of war, especially that mockery of making war for the sake of peace. The image of this divine insanity of unholy communion is a tortured Jesus dying on the cross: abandoned by God, or consumed by God? If you are to live happily on this grief-stricken planet, you will have to wrestle with the holy question and seeming contradiction: Is God fully present or fully absent in all the evils of life's ten thousand times ten thousands of vicious, crucifixion-like tribulations?

While you grapple with Mystery, take heart that the task of living joyfully is not impossible if you embrace the reality that everything is saturated with the Divine. Faith is the source of sight, as is love. And love and faith are the source of joy. Regardless of how enormous the evil of the day, how dishonestly corrupt the government or Church, one must continue living in joy since we trust in the law of karma, or the law of the harvest as it is known in Christianity. As Paul taught in 2 Corinthians 9:10, that law says that the one who supplies the seed to the one who sows will increase the harvest of righteousness. As disciples of the Master of

Peace, lavishly sow seeds of nonviolence, and opposition to war and killing, with trust and confidence that God will produce the harvest of righteousness of justice and peace. Along with trust you must—like a very good farmer—be patient for the time of the harvest. Living in trust includes fidelity to the mystery that God has chosen to dwell among us while we wait for the harvest of the grapes of wrath. Meanwhile those who deceive, oppress, and engage in iniquity will be visited by the harvest of their evil deeds.

The presence of God in our waiting is like a letter from someone you love. When you read a letter from someone you love, that person—even while invisible—becomes present as you read the words he or she has written to you. Christian belief is that Jesus of Nazareth was the Word of God made flesh, and that in him were experienced God's love, mercy, and pardon. Jesus, however, was not the first word made flesh. At the dawn of creation, the Creator spoke, "Let there be rivers, forests, fish, and wild beasts." To read those love letters is to be in the presence of the invisible Divine Mystery both in the spellbinding beauty of a delicate lily and the awesomely disturbing destruction of a hurricane.

All too easily do the misty cataracts of custom cloud our vision, and absent-mindedness blinds us to our beliefs. If only we could see with faith all creation as a living expression of the Divine Mystery, we would be shaken awake by "disturbing joy," to paraphrase Wordsworth. To be divinely disturbed out of our perpetual sleepwalking, so as to be disturbed by joy, requires a healing of our blindness that no medical procedure or sacrament can provide. As habit blinds,

so habit heals. A ceaseless craving to see with those
Spirit-eyes that enlighten the darkness of every sadness
and misery reveals within the hidden presence of joy.
This craving, like all addictions, needs constant renewal.
Prayer feeds the obsession. The shorter the prayer the
better since it can more easily become habit. A potent
one, when prayed with faith, is the plea of the blind
beggar of Jericho in the Gospel of Luke, "Lord, please
let me see."

As faith opened his eyes, so addictive desire to see
can open your eyes to what lies beneath the drab surface
of all things. If you desire to uncover the hidden treasure in the mundanely commonplace, repeat those five
potent words as frequently as possible, making them a
perpetual prayer. Since prayer is also the key to unravel-
ing the seeming contradictions of the Mystery of God,
this reflection concludes with the following prayer:

Oh Mystery of Mysteries,
whom I clumsily call "God,"
you are beyond all images,
definitions, and explanations,
yet my heart longs to feel you
within me, and wherever I am.

This doubter aches to believe that
you chose before the sun's birth
to abide in all of creation:
night's darkness and day's light,
in human good and in our evil,
in nature's beauties and disasters.

I believe, but help my unbelief.

six

the mysticism of the
smile

While laughter is a human sign of happiness and joy, seldom, if ever, in religious art is the fully human Jesus Christ ever shown laughing or even smiling! In none of the four gospels of his life is it said that he ever laughed or smiled. The Native American Apache maintain that laughter is the essence of being human and of being alive. The Apache creation story tells how the creator prepared the very first human to come alive by giving him abilities to talk, walk and run, think and plan, and look and hear. While all these were good, something critical was missing. So the creator withheld life from his human creation until he could do just one more thing—laugh! So man laughed and laughed and laughed. And then the creator said, "Now at last are you fit to be alive."

While called to live in joy, we are not required to greet every event in our lives with laughter. On this woefully wounded earth such unrestricted delight as is expressed by laughter isn't possible. However, not laughter but a smile is the most common expression of those living in joy. A smile, that uniquely human facial expression, is created by the upward curving of the corners of the mouth along with the accompanying (and impossible to fake) twinkle in the eyes. A smile is a facial message of friendliness, delight, satisfaction, and amusement, as well as the sheer joy of enjoyment.

While the disciples of Jesus of Galilee never recorded that the Master even smiled, the disciples of Buddha have spoken of his blissful smile. Paintings and statues of Buddha do show him smiling, unlike solemn-faced images of Christ. Since smiling is extraordinarily rare in depictions of divine or savior figures, Buddhist scholars are careful to distinguish the smiles of Buddha. They list six classes of laughter, from the most sublime in a descending scale to the most uncouth and crude. They begin with *sita*, a faint, almost undetectable smile, which is followed by *hasita*, a smile that involves the slightest movement of the lips, revealing only a glimpse of the teeth. The third classification is *vihasita*, a broad smile reaching from ear to ear that is often accompanied by laughter. Next comes *upanhasita*, a broad-faced smile that is accompanied by some laughter. Fifth is *apahasita*, a smile accompanied by loud laughter so intense as to bring tears. Finally, in last place, is *aithasita*, the belly laughter that is so boisterous as to rock the entire body.

This wonderful Buddhist catalog of smiles was influenced by the ideals of aristocratic superiority, where only the first two classes were proper for those with refinement. In those circles, Buddha is shown only smiling with that faint, almost undetectable *sita* smile. If artists ever begin to depict the joy of Jesus, they will no doubt also limit his expression to a *sita* smile. The next two classes of smiles of moderate laughter are those ascribed to the merchant or the average person. The last two classes of excessive and vulgar laughter are reserved to the lower, coarse, and uncouth classes, such as peasants. Yet Jesus of Nazareth was no aristocrat but a peasant and common workman, so if he laughed, did he do so in a boisterous way? If he did, would a raucous, full-bodied laughter diminish in any way his holiness—his intimate union with the all holy one?

While Christianity lacks religious images of laughing alone, or even smiling saints, Buddhism has that notoriously happy, saintly, old and fat, potbellied Pu-Tai. This famous laughing Buddha is a statue often found at the entrances of Chinese restaurants. He is always depicted laughing with great gusto, as are those other jolly Buddhist holy men, Han-shan and Shih-te. The saintly tradition of Pu-Tai tells of how he spurned the cloister claustrophobia of monasteries to wander the open road. He went dancing down the road to some inaudible music, played with little children in the village streets, and delighted them by acting the crazy fool with joyful, mad humor. Pu-Tai, both a wise and holy man, knew that for those living in a village or a monastery the greatest temptation was the craving of the hungry old ego for respect or to be important. Old Pu-Tai was unconcerned if his fat potbelly didn't make him look saintly, nor that he was the target of the laughter of children and adults. By wild, silly buffoonery he achieved the prize of holiness he sought with such carefree passion.

a **cheerful cure**
for xenophobia

Smiling is also a sure remedy for xenophobia—the fear of strangers, especially those of different colored skin than yours, or who speak a foreign language. Smiling at any stranger immediately indicates that you don't consider that person as dangerous or an enemy, but an unknown friend. The unrecognized friend is your Beloved, who promised that whenever you reach to assist those in need, he would be the one you helped, even if only with a smile. To those hungry for welcome and acceptance, a smiling face is food and drink. Befriending the hidden friend requires lifelong faith since the Beloved will not be unmasked in this lifetime, but only after your death when you learn to your surprise at whom you were really smiling. So as you make your way along the street, waiting in line at the checkout counter, or in any human encounter, smile as authentically as possible at everyone you meet. This smile is a leap or feat of faith since everyone isn't naturally attractive or friendly looking.

Natural smiles and frowns are easily distinguished from artificial ones, whose intent is actually to disguise instead of reveal. Good manners, regardless of your true feelings, always dictate and sanction smiling when greeting people. The negative opposite of a smile is a frown, which signals displeasure, confusion, anger, or aversion. A frown can also be both natural and artificial. A manufactured frown is often used to intimidate, or "browbeat," which is a delightful word that describes the use of the weapon of a wrinkled brow to bully others. While smiles and frowns come and go on the human face depending upon various circumstances, hidden beneath every human face is an abiding smile or frown. Years of deep dissatisfaction with yourself and discontentment with the cards that fate has dealt you in the game of life fashion an abiding internal frown. And the reverse is true, of course; years of striving to live joyfully etch your soul with a smile. Often unbeknown to their owners, one of these two internal expressions is being continuously expressed, even if it does not appear externally. Scan reflectively the faces of people passing you on the sidewalk, fellow passengers on a bus, or those sitting in a church or a doctor's office, and you will see etched there the interior frown or smile that many of them wear on their souls.

Those who always appear to be sad may suffer from a hidden medical deficiency. In 2001, a series of

advertisements appeared in Boston newspapers that
read, "Are you extremely moody? Do you often feel out
of control? Are your relationships painful and difficult?" Mary Zanarini, a Harvard psychologist and one
of the nation's leading researchers in personality disor-
ders, placed these unusual advertisements in the newspapers. She was seeking volunteers to be part of the
testing of an experimental treatment for those suffering
from depression and like difficulties. The treatment
involved the consumption of omega-3 fatty acids found
in fish. Research has discovered that these fatty acids
help to ward off depression and a range of other neuro-
logical problems. The brain, being 60 percent fat,
requires a healthy supply of omega-3 for proper func-
tioning. Studies indicate that by acting like a neutron
fertilizer, omega-3 boosts levels of the chemical sero-
tonin found in the brain. I have used this medical
research as a way of acknowledging that some people,
for genetic or biological reasons, may actually be unable
to live joyfully. Strive as hard as they can, pray with as
much faith as possible, the chemistry of their brains
creates a state of moodiness and sadness that makes
them incapable of living a joyful life. However, for the
majority of us, it is possible to live a joyful life—by fer-
vently desiring it, by forming proper attitudes toward
life's troubles, and by cooperation with the abundant
graces of God.

Those who have a happy soul don't have to wear a
smile on the outside or always look cheerful to be recognized as happy, contented people. If enduring discontent
and dissatisfaction creates an inner frown, what creates a

smiling soul? Is it created in those who have been blessed with the good fortune of being born into a loving family, have inherited great physical and intellectual gifts, or have been successful in life? Apparently not, since many so blessed by natural beauty and talents— the stars of sports and Hollywood, or those who have acquired billions of dollars in business—do not live contented, happy lives! If not beauty or talents, is the source of the inner smile some cheerful combination of chemicals, a lucky roll of the dice of the DNA genes, or the result of being nurtured in a pleasant, affirming home environment?

Obviously something deeper than your DNA or natural gifts is responsible for living a joyful life. Part of that secret is found in our uniquely human ability to smile. Feelings of joy or happiness can both precede as well as follow the facial expression of a smile! When you smile without feeling happy you'll find that you actually begin to feel happier, more contented, and more relaxed. As a way of awakening the hidden pres- ence of Divine Joy, experiment with smiling frequently, regardless of the circumstances. Smile, especially when you find yourself in a neutral life-space that is neither good nor bad. Experiment with smiling frequently throughout your day: upon entering the supermarket and while shopping; waiting for stalled traffic to move again; or upon entering a room. Smile frequently also when you're working alone and see if you don't begin to experience the joy of life.

Another unique, almost magical—if not miraculous— aspect of the human smile is its ability to transform some unpleasant negative mood whenever we feel angry or upset. The grace of the sacrament of the smile is found in its presence that unconsciously asks, "What's so funny?" If we have pursued living in joy with passion, prayed for that grace, and engaged frequently in the sacrament of the smile, we're likely to answer, "Hey Self, how could you be so upset by such a trivial issue?"

eight

my smile does
magnify the Lord

Mary of Nazareth, aware that she carried the hidden presence of the one who she believed was God's Anointed, sang out joyfully, "My soul magnifies the Lord . . . for the Mighty One has done great things for me!"[1] Her beautiful canticle of rejoicing is frequently prayed and is also a daily canticle of the sunset prayer hour of Vespers. Her jubilant song also asks an interesting question: "Why are there not statues or paintings of an ecstatically rejoicing Mary, the Mother of God?"

Why this void of any smiling icons of the Magnificat Madonna? (*Magnificat* is the old familiar name for this prayer. It comes from the Latin for the opening words, "My soul magnifies the Lord!" *Magnificat anima mea Dominium.*) I am personally unaware of any rejoicing Madonnas. Perhaps they do exist, and I've just never seen them. It seems that the best we can ever hope to see on the face of the peasant Virgin Mary, like on Buddha, is an aristocratically polite *sita* smile. Our western ascetic and sober Christian concept of what constitutes holiness doesn't allow for a laughing or even smiling Mary or Jesus.

A laughing Madonna would indicate not only that her soul was mightily enlarging, exposing the Divine Presence for all to see, but also that it was dynamically alive. Souls can be vivaciously alive and also dormant, slumbering or dead to the world, as the folk expression so vividly describes. The power of laughter and joy to awaken a dormant soul is a Native American belief. An earlier reflection in this book contained the delightful Apache story of creation where the creator made humans come fully alive by giving them the ability to laugh. Among the Navajo, a newborn baby is carefully observed for his or her soul moment, that mystical moment when the baby first laughs. The Navajo believe that the soul, which in their native language is the same word as wind, as in Hebrew, enters the body sometime soon after birth. When the baby first laughs, it signals that glorious moment when the soul has finally been attached to the infant's body. This soul-fusing-with-body event that occurs when a child first laughs takes place around three and a half months after birth.

We acknowledge that sometimes people appear to be alive but are actually brain-dead, and so not properly living persons. Can there be a parallel condition when people appear alive and yet are soul-dead? One's spirit can become exhausted by overexposure to excessive noise and activity, worry and stress. While present physically, the person is inactive and unresponsive within. This soul-slumber isn't restricted to times of intense involvement in secular activities; even times of prayer and worship can and often do induce soul-coma by their hypnotizing repetitiveness. When the soul is comatose, prayer quickly becomes mechanical, and communal worship becomes little more than soulless, robotic ritual actions.

Exhausted souls, being unconscious, are unaware that they are not in attendance to the rest of the body. It is the duty of the mind to frequently rouse them to life. The best advice to maintain a wakeful soul is a healthy lifestyle of living in joy. Rejoicing stimulates the soul and may be one of the reasons we are invited to strive to be always, forever and a day, joyful. Since it seems humanly impossible to be joyful in every single circumstance in life, your soul can easily nod off and take spiritual catnaps.

To ensure that your prayer and worship of God are physically and therefore mystically alive instead of motorized, consider the following introduction to prayer. Before praying privately or with others, even at mealtimes, which can easily become mechanized by routine or eagerness to begin the meal, pause to take a couple of deep breaths, and then smile broadly. Since smiling while praying seems so incongruent, you may find it too embarrassing to smile at such a somber, pious moment. Aware that a grinning prayer can raise eyebrows and form frowns, you may wish to piously bow your head before you pray so you don't have to explain "what's so entertaining"!

Every prayer is a preparation to "pray always," to live prayerfully so times of formal prayer act as porter-prayers to usher you into being fully, soulfully engaged in living prayer. How we conclude these usher-prayers then is important especially in regard to the uninter-rupted prayer of living joyfully. To ensure your soul's alertness as you enter into that living prayer of grati-tude and joy, replace the conventional conclusion of "Amen" with a broad smile or even a chuckle.

Mary the Mother of God has that beautiful title of the Queen of Saints, and a laughing Madonna would be a great boost for a long-overdue change in the commun-ion of saints. Sadly, those declared to have officially joined the heavenly hosts always appear as sober or pious-faced saints. You see their unhappy faces painted in the ceiling frescoes of the great basilicas of Rome and chiseled in the stone in the carvings of paradise found over the doors of the great medieval cathedrals. Sad saints are truly sad. But don't expect the appear-ance of smiling Madonnas anytime soon, since suffer-ing and sorrow are our preferred characteristics we attribute to Mary the Mother of God and to Jesus along with the saints.

[1] Luke 1:46, 49

the **weeping** Madonna

Mary's canticle of soul-exploding joy and gratitude is daily recited in the sunset prayer of
Vespers. The timeless ritual for beginning this
joyous hymn is to trace the Sign of the Cross upon one-
self as you say the opening words, "My soul does magnify God since he who is mighty has done great things
for me, Holy is God's Name." Making the Sign of the
Cross as you begin her song of joy is fitting, since that
sinister sign will overshadow her joys of motherhood.
This canticle is an ideal prayer for those women suffering difficulties in their marriages or the struggles and
pains of their children.

While we lack statues of a smiling, rejoicing
Mother of God, we have no shortage of statues of Our
Lady of Sorrows. And frequent are the reported sight-
ings of statues of the Madonna that miraculously weep

tears of sorrow. Mary as the Sorrowful Mother is a familiar image to Roman Catholics, since it once was a popular devotion among women in the United States. In various forms it is still common with Mexican Americans as "*Nuestra Señora de los Dolores,*" and also in Latin America and Europe. The appeal of this devotion to the Mother of Sorrows in third world countries is understandable. In those poor countries mothers endure the painful anguish of helplessly watching their children suffer sickness without medicines or proper care. They are living sorrowful mothers whose grief comes from having to raise their children in dire poverty and hunger, and see them die early deaths.

In religious art the Suffering Mother is depicted as a grieving woman, her face etched in great pain and her hands clasped together at her breast. In paintings and statues of the crucifixion, this image of the grief-stricken mother of Jesus is depicted standing at the foot of his cross. Another image of the Sorrowful Mother depicts her with seven swords sticking out of her heart! The origin of this sword-pierced, grief-stricken Madonna is found in the words of old Simeon to Mary, "and a sword will pierce your own soul too."[1] He spoke these words to her at the time of her Mosaic purification ritual, after which he blessed her infant, predicting that to his own people the child would be a sign of contradiction. This sword-piercing heart prediction is usually interpreted that she as his mother could not remain unaffected by the hostile reactions to her son, including his crucifixion.

It is understandable that women were and are drawn to this devotion of Our Lady of Sorrows, since they identify with her as a suffering mother to whom they might turn amid the struggles and tribulations of their marriages and families. "To rejoice always" is not an easy imperative for those mothers who have identified themselves so intimately—almost physically—with the sufferings, trials, and misfortunes of their children. Mothers fret and worry about their children, even when as adults they marry and have children of their own. Some mothers feel a maternal obligation to simultaneously suffer in their children's sorrows as if their birthing pains were intended to be lifelong. So to ask such women to identity with a smiling Madonna or to live joyful lives can easily be seen as an attack on their motherhood.

Since mothers share in the sufferings of the children of their womb, those prophetic words of old Simeon could be appropriately addressed to every mother at the conclusion of her infant's baptism. Not simply mothering but all parenting is painful, as every mother and father knows. Still they are called to live lives of joy while enduring the sorrows of their children. Whatever your state in life—married, single, vowed religious, or ordained—it is essential to find a balance between joy and those sorrows that seem so unavoidable in this life. This balancing act is easier if you live the art of the famous three: giving thanks constantly, praying always, and rejoicing always.

Give thanks constantly by expressing true gratitude for every small daily domestic kindness. Pray always by living as consciously as possible in the presence of God as that mystery unfolds within your home. And rejoice always by searching for something good, the potential of happiness, hidden in every event—even events that are sorrowful. This last discovery of a joy hidden in some misfortune requires trusting God. Faith encourages you to open yourself to God's creative ability to convert darkness into light, to generate life out of death, to convert anger into peace and sorrow into joy.

I recently found a confirmation of the power of this trust in an unexpected place: a Chinese fortune cookie! Unfolding the small slip of paper, I was delighted to read, "Every adversity carries with it the seed of an equal or greater benefit." The harvest of these seeds of joy-laced blessings that are hidden in the darkness of suffering does not appear instantly or miraculously, regardless of the depth of your faith. Rather, as the wisdom of my fortune cookie implied, Each adversity holds a seed of some benefit of equal or even greater joy. To reap that equal or even greater good fortune requires trustingly nurturing that seed into an Easter Lily of Joy.

[1] Luke 2:35

the mother of joy
is trust

Faithful trust is the mother of the joy that Jesus promised, and also of his freedom from anxieties and fear. To live a joyous life challenges your faith and your conviction in God's endlessly unbounded and personal love for you. A deep faith sends up green sprouts into every aspect of your daily life. With time these grow into branches that bend low, heavy with fruit.

Mary's song of gratitude rejoices extraordinarily in the God who placed her in the embarrassing circumstance of being pregnant without being married! So, regardless of your circumstances, positive or negative, let your smile externalize the joy of your awareness of Divine Mystery within you and also of the hidden purposes unfolding in your life. In spite of what may be the unpleasant circumstances of your day, and of how seemingly absent God is from your life, sing a canticle of joyous gratitude. You can compose an actual prayer-song, or you can simply sing a silent song by smiling. Let your smile be an expression of your joyful gratitude and, like Mary's actions, let it magnify the hidden presence of God within you. An example of such a Prayer of Magnifying might be:

O God, you, the constantly invisible One,
have done great things for me this day.
May my gratitude-soaked soul magnify you
so expansively that by my smile all will know
of your abiding presence in me
and in them.

Rejoice also that you are no clay vessel or tabernacle holding the Nameless One, for along with Jesus, you also can say, "The Father and I are one." Let your belief in that intimate unity between you and Christ, and your awesome unity with the Divine Mystery, become so real that it will be unbreakable by sin or human mistakes. We are conditioned by religious instruction—if not by our own inability to believe in such an impossible reality—to experience God's indwelling and that of Christ as something "spiritual," akin to that which happens in the reception of Holy Communion. If, however, the presence of God is so integrated in us as to saturate the totality of our person, would not such a reality elicit from us ecstatic joy and unflappable conviction? Only a great personal love for you could explain God's desire to be infused in every cell of your body. Even to begin to grasp the implications of being so loved should stun us with drunken joyfulness.

Unquestioned conviction of this divine indwelling would erase itching worries about tomorrow and wipe clean the grime of daily anxieties and fretfulness. Jesus' taproot belief was that he and the Father were one, and from that pulsating taproot arose upward branches reaching into his daily life. Because of his conviction in this inner reality, he could call us also to join with him in living with unflinching conviction in God's abiding love and care for our every need.

When your core belief is your intimate unity with God that then branches off into every other religious belief, great things are possible! This core belief will manifest itself by unnatural and unpredictable behavior: responding nonviolently when attacked, returning kindness when abused, and loving those who dislike and even hate you. Such radical, unnatural responses are not piously good; they are God-like. Indeed they are acts of God! Only those with great faith can "unnaturally" be loving, kind, and nonviolent. Ironically, by these unnatural behaviors we discover our true nature—our Godhood.

Belief and faith are not the same things. Faith is usually something we hold to be true, while belief is a trust wedded to conviction. Like all nuptials, this marriage is a union created by love. For the Master, the cardinal rule of life was a total love of God: body, soul, mind, and heart, since only by such an encompassing loving of

God do we become like God. Love then has the power to awaken us to who we truly are, and this mystical awareness should skyrocket us into bliss.

Not by some mystical vision, some sudden enlightened burst of enthralling energy, do we find the source of living joyfully. It is rather by living day-by-day our common, ordinary life, trusting in and conscious of God's intimate union with us, that we find the undying source of happiness. Yet no other thought could be more audacious, so religiously bizarre than to actually allow all your thoughts, attitudes, and behaviors to flow from the belief that God and you are one! Only the mad or possessed would dare claim such impossible intimacy!

eleven

the **hidden** presence

The presence of God within yourself and others isn't considered bizarre or insane by those in the East. Hindus acknowledge this indwelling of the Divine with a simple but profound ritual upon greeting another person. Instead of our custom of shaking hands and saying, "Hello," Hindus fold their hands together in front of their chest and with a slight bow of the head say, "*Namaste.*" They acknowledge the presence of the Divine Mystery both in themselves and in others by this single word, which can be translated as, "I reverence the Divine Spirit in you which is also in me." What is customary in India or among Hindus would appear as esoteric and inappropriate for us in this country, but an adaptation of *namaste* could provide a potent ritual of remembrance. Upon greeting or even encountering another person, to slightly incline your

head in a silent bow can be a personal way of acknowledging God's indwelling in another. To consciously perform this simple ritual can also be a reminder of the
fact that the same presence of God is within you.

Bowing is an ageless gesture of greeting one who is
superior to you, but in a democracy where all are supposed to be equal, it can seem demeaning. A slight bow
of the head as a sign of humility when greeting any
other person is also a reminder of one's servant status
as a disciple of the Master. He was very explicit in his
demand that those who followed him were to be ser-
vants to one another, even using the word "slave." A
slight bow of the head can be a profession of faith and
a prayer adoring the Presence of God in those whom
you encounter, and also a humble reminder of your
duty to be of service to them as best you can.

Along with this simple greeting ritual, to live with a
joyous spirit requires not a simple bow, but a profound
plummet! Thomas Merton wrote in his *New Seeds of
Contemplation*,

> If you descend into the depths of your own
>   spirit . . .
> and arrive somewhere near the center of
>   what you are,
> you are confronted with the inescapable truth,
> at the very root of your existence, you are in
>   constant
> and immediate and inescapable contact with the
> infinite power of God.

And I might add, at the very root of your existence is a bubbling spring of inextinguishable joy!

To acknowledge the daily social consequences of this indwelling presence of God that saturates every atom and fiber of our bodies is awe inspiring and encouraging. When one suffers from some respiratory virus, like the common head cold, rejoicing is possible, since the symptoms of the sickness touch only your outer surface, since God dwelling within is immune to all disease. When you detect in the mirror those sad signs of aging, you can rejoice, since that deterioration is only skin-deep. The Divine Mystery united to you is eternally youthful and ageless. Whenever you feel confronted by the imminent presence of some dire threat or menacing evil, a happy spirit is still possible, since the Sacred Undefeatable One within you has been victorious over every evil in the world, even death itself.

When bedridden with some illness, fearful over some approaching event, or directly confronted by some trouble, you have to descend quickly to those roots of your soul to cause that deep fount of joy in your roots to bubble up to the surface. This holy descent takes but a few profoundly trust-filled moments. Once you feel you've reached your deepest depths, come to a quiet rest among the tangled roots of your being and inhale deeply the abundant, fertile power of the Divine Presence. Then ascend as quickly as you descended to joyously face in a new way whatever threatens your peace. Do so with confidence, for if God is with you, in you, and intimately one with you, who or what can be against you?

If you wish to live joyously regardless of circumstances, develop the habit of frequent descents to be nourished by that abiding holy communion with God. To be frequently in a day in consecrated constant communion requires only going into yourself. Those who practice these daily frequent descents and ascents can smile with that singular joy of which the Master promised, ". . . no one will take . . . from you."

twelve

in **your identity**
is your inheritance

The source of living joyously is found in, of all places, your identity! Unless you suffer from amnesia, you know who you are, or at least you think you know who you are. And you are the most important person in the world! Before you reject outright that last statement, consider your daily thoughts. The human mind must think hundreds of millions of thoughts each day. And of all these millions of thoughts, are not the most frequent ones about yourself? Unconsciously the mind is bombarded by zillions of messages from your senses, nerves, and organs. You are even the central character or witness of events in your night's dreams.

The ancient Greek philosophers taught, "Know thyself." Yet the one thing you know the least about is yourself. This fact explains the need for psychologists, therapists, counselors, and good friends who all help you understand the mystery of your true identity. Added to your sexual, social, and psychological identity is also a spiritual identity. To "know thyself" as a child of God is perhaps the easiest spiritual identity to grasp, since everyone has been a child. Your spiritual identity becomes more complex if you have been baptized a Christian. By this water ritual the Spirit makes the baptized into a new creation. The baptized child or adult has become "one in Christ" and can say with Paul, "I no longer live, but Christ lives in me." This entirely new Christ-identity catapults those who take it seriously into an even deeper identity problem.

However, for the majority of believers, baptism doesn't create any identity problems. For them it is simply a ritual that removes original sin and makes them a member of a certain church. But having a Christian identity cannot in itself be the source of daily zestful enjoyment, at least for the majority of Christians whom I know. If baptism makes you a disciple of Jesus the Master, then discipleship could be a very significant identity that implies being included in the Last Will of the Master.

The author of the Gospel of John relates that on the night before his death Jesus told his disciples of their inheritance. With only a few words he bequeaths a legacy of unimaginably fabulous wealth, one that all the money in the world can't buy—happiness. "That my joy may be yours, and that your joy may be complete." This lavish inheritance would be theirs and that of the future disciples of the coming ages.

One task of every disciple who has ever emerged from the baptismal pool is to claim his or her inheritance by living it. What did Jesus mean in wishing that this inherited joy might be complete, that it was now lacking in some way? Complete can mean accomplished, inclusive, and comprehensive, which implies far-reaching. Perhaps this last expression holds a clue to that wish Jesus placed on his inheritance—you cannot use it for private delight. Rather it must be inclusive and far-reaching.

As disciples of the Divine Joy, we sow seeds of joy everywhere we go and in everyone we encounter. It is easy to be simply a child of God, or even a faithful member of a church, but to be a true disciple is not easy. Yet discipleship carries the promise of inheriting a bountiful legacy. So ponder the possibility that as a disciple of Jesus you have an unclaimed inheritance. Stories abound of vast sums of money and property left to gather dust on courthouse shelves since the inheritors have failed to claim their legacies or are simply unaware that they have been named as benefactors in a will. That Jesus left a will before he died may surprise many, and they may be even more surprised to learn that they have a copy of that will in their bible: "I speak these things in the world so that they may have my joy made complete in themselves."[1]

[1] John 17:13

joy **robbers**

In our increasingly fast-paced world, nothing seems more frustrating than having to wait, since it is such a waste of time! Waiting in traffic, waiting in a long line at a checkout counter, waiting on the telephone when you've been put "on hold," or having to wait for someone tardy for an appointment. These difficult waiting situations become thieves of our happiness. If you desire to live a joyful life, you will be required to learn that un-American art of being pleasantly content, even if at the moment that happens to be wasting time. Being pleasingly satisfied when your flight has been delayed or road repair work brings you to a standstill means you've escaped from those crooks of the clock that steal your time, and with it, your joy. So how do you escape from these and other pickpockets of joy?

Joy robbers are everywhere. Unlike bank bandits, they brazenly do not wear masks to hide their faces. The faces of these criminals are clearly recognizable, for they are the faces on our watches and clocks. These round, featureless faces ringed in numbers are not the thieves themselves, but only the scenes of the robberies where the crimes take place. While these ever-elusive thieves can't be arrested or imprisoned, they can be disarmed. In the morning before you put on your wristwatch, pause, holding it briefly in the palm of your hand, and pray. If you do not wear a wristwatch, then take your bedside clock and hold it in your hand and pray.

O You, who are timeless,
thank you for the twenty-four new hours
you've generously loaned, without interest,
to me this day.
All the minutes and hours of my clocks
belong to you, the timeless and eternal One.

Remind me to never call a single moment
of it "my time" to spend for my personal use.
Inspire me to rejoice when I'm unexpectedly
asked to spend some of it on others' needs.
Help me count those occasions as blessed moments.

Yielding to what is beyond my control,
I accept what appears to be a waste of time,
        yet in truth is that priceless gift of prayer that
you prize so much—

the Prayer of Surrender to you
and your holy will for me this day.

I encourage you to create your own brief prayer as
you strap your watch to your wrist, something as brief
as:

Thank you for the hours of this day—
a gift I've been given to give away.

Commit your prayer to memory so that it flows
freely as you pray it at the beginning of the day or
whenever you are forced to wait. In this time of frequently being frustrated by having to wait, let your
silent wristwatch be like a chapel bell calling you to
prayer time.

fourteen

the **sound** of mu**s**ic

This reflection isn't about that charming Broadway musical and hit film about the Von Trapp family of Austria, but about the source of the ability to live a life of joy. What incentive moves you to keep the Ten Commandments or engage in the works of mercy to the poor and afflicted that the Master called us to perform? Historically, the Ten Commandments were kept out of fear of the dire consequences of breaking them—going to hell. Since, in the modern world, few any longer fear personal eternal damnation, the threat of hell-fire has ceased being an incinerating incentive to live morally good lives. Once considered as the reward only for those living a good, if not holy, life, heaven is now commonly believed to be the ultimate destination of just about everyone. So what then is the incentive to be morally good, law-abiding, and generous to the poor and disadvantaged? Today common decency seems to have become the prime motivator for truthfulness in speech, honesty in business, kindness to strangers, and donating to those in need. Low-grade guilt is often the incentive for the middle class to give money to the poor, not to mention the additional bonus of IRS tax deductions.

However, the best incentive for living a morally good and generous life is not fear, but music! The word *incentive* comes from the Latin word for singing, *incinere*. The most compelling motivator isn't the compulsion of law, fear of punishment, or even spiritual gain, but that prehistoric talent that has all but disappeared from daily life today—singing! Yet the majority of us are fearful, or at best very hesitant, to sing solo and especially *a cappella*, other than for "Happy Birthday." This was not always the case. In previous ages, workers sang songs to accompany their labors, when carrying heavy loads, picking cotton, or driving spikes on the railroad. These songs, sung by gangs of laborers or by individuals working alone, helped to relieve the heavy burden of their work and to pass the time. Soldiers once marched into war singing songs to rally their courage, and in today's boot camp recruits sing or chant as they drill. The old adage to "whistle while you work" carries the same underlying incentive that music or a melody has the power to enhance whatever you do.

African American slaves sang in the evenings to ease the pains of their slavery and backbreaking labor. When they gathered in small black churches, they sang for a different reason—to express joy and hope. During their nonviolent protests against racial discrimination in the 1960s, the freedom marchers sang, "We Shall Overcome." It embodied, as did so many other African American spirituals, their ironclad, joyful conviction that God had guaranteed them success in their efforts to become truly equal citizens. As they struggled with disgraceful, subhuman treatment, being limited to only menial jobs, it was their singing that gave voice to God's promises of freedom. The joy in these songs was no ordinary delight, for it was a joy stronger than the shame and humiliation of being treated as less than human. It was an "always" joy.

Mahalia Jackson's powerful rendition of the old classic "His Eye Is on the Sparrow" expresses both African Americans' joyful hope and their passionate desire for freedom.

Why should I feel discouraged
Why should the shadows come
Why should my heart feel lonely
And long for heaven and home
When Jesus is my portion, a constant friend
I sing because I'm happy
I sing because I'm free.

The lyrics of this hymn were originally written as a poem by Civilla Martin. In 1905 she and her husband were in Elmira, New York, and became good friends with a uniquely joyful couple, Mr. and Mrs. Doolittle. What made this couple's unflappable joy unique was that Mrs. Doolittle had been bedridden for close to twenty years. Her husband was an incurable cripple who had to struggle to work from a wheelchair. Civilla was amazed at how they were able to be always so joyful and bright, in spite of their crippling afflictions. When she questioned Mrs. Doolittle about how they were able to do this, Mrs. Doolittle replied, "His eye is on the sparrow, and I know He watches me." Her simple yet profound reply inspired Civilla to compose a poem about the source of their joy. She then sent it to Charles Gabriel, who set it to music.

This song, along with other African American spirituals, is but another version of "Joy to the World." They were written as and remain living encores of that old Christmas carol. They were not pious hymns but victory songs of ironclad conviction.

> Jesus is my entrance to God's heart,
> where no dark shadows ever fall.
> Jesus is my stead, my lover, companion in life,
> and there ain't no chains ever made strong enough
> to hold me—because I'm free!

> Title Unknown

While in our white, Anglo-Saxon culture singing is no longer a part of daily life, especially singing *a cappella*, it is possible to sing when you can hear the sound of music! Ironically this music can't be heard with those ears on either side of your head, since it's soul or inner music. It is the heart that hears, and entices you to sing along. This soul music, which is the most compelling of all enticements, is hidden inside another song that the wise are continuously chanting: the endless hymn of happy gratitude. Those who are always grateful actually hear the song of the Divine Beloved singing in the melodic sign language of endless gifts: life, love, friendship, physical and mental health, family, and home. They hear it in every beauty and wonder in the world. Let that mystic melody you hear with your senses—the gifts your eyes touch upon, the gifts your hands feel, and tastes and smells all around you—arouse you to sing two songs to the gift giver. The first is the song of praying always, giving thanks in all circumstances, and always living a joyous life. The second song is the inaudible song of kindness to the stranger, compassion to the unfortunate, and unconditional acceptance to those who suffer discrimination.

A concluding thought about our terror at being asked to sing *a cappella* even when our soul hears the melody of the Beloved: the musical notation *a cappella*, besides meaning "unaccompanied," also means "singing in the style of old church music." In the early centuries of Christianity, musical instruments of any kind were forbidden, since only the unaccompanied human voice was considered proper for prayer and worship of God. So when you're alone at home or driving in your car, don't hesitate to sing solo, since you're just praying in the style of old church music and prayer.

fifteen

sing a **happy song**

This reflection continues the previous one, and regardless of your singing abilities, consider singing a part of your day. Along with its incentive powers, singing has healing ones. While Alzheimer's disease continues to defy a cure, singing songs appears to assist those suffering from this horrible illness. Alzheimer's patients can become depressed with the approach of darkness at the end of the day, or when they move from one place to another. They can even become very fearful when visited by family members whom they now no longer recognize. Some caregivers find that singing old, familiar songs upon entering a patient's room greatly eases the patient's anxiety. Regardless of the subconscious connection with particular songs, perhaps Alzheimer's patients feel that if someone is singing, everything must be all right. For those who object that they can't sing, doctors advise that they recite or read poetry, since it is almost like singing.

Sadly, the basic human trait of singing that once accompanied all forms of work and play has now largely disappeared from daily life for us in the so-called "developed" world. Perhaps being able to hear the finest talent on television, radio, and CDs intimidates the average person from singing. Musical technology has created a preference for listening to professionals sing instead of the average person singing bits and pieces of songs. Everyone can sing to some degree. So don't worry about the sound of your voice—God created both crows and canaries, and apparently finds each of their voices divinely appealing. Make today a little Easter and resurrect your primal human gift by singing at least once a day. To rephrase an old adage, "A song a day keeps the blues away." This encouragement to sing to yourself throughout the day and at certain occasions will be a great assistance in your efforts to live in joy.

Having been born and raised in the Great American Depression of the 1930s, I grew up hearing the marvelous healing songs of that period on the radio and in motion pictures. I intentionally use the adjective *healing*, since with millions out of work and no hope of finding a job, the grim poverty, hunger, and homelessness—these years were truly a depressing era. Recently I came across a quotation from the Buffalo Evening News dated 1931:

Middleton, N.Y. Dec. 24
Attracted by smoke from the chimney of a sup-
posedly empty summer cottage, the Sullivan
County Constable found a young couple starving. Three days without food, the wife, who is
twenty-three years old, was hardly able to walk.
They went into the cottage, preferring to starve
rather than beg.

The extent of the poverty and hunger of these hard
times was also reported in a statement by the Child's
Bureau of the Labor Department on June 18, 1931:

City schools revealed today that 11,000 hungry
children are being fed by their teachers . . . [who
themselves] are seriously handicapped by the failure of the Board of Education to pay them.

In those years of the Great Depression, homeless
men and women numbering in the millions stood in
long breadlines or waited stoically outside soup
kitchens, defeated, discouraged, hopeless. They were
also deeply ashamed, like that young couple, to be
forced to come asking for public aid. My own parents,
like the millions of others who struggled through those
years, were strong people who were made even stronger
by their determined endurance of these hard times.

As a child during those difficult times, the happy,
hope-filled songs of those Depression days are tattooed
on my memory even to this day. Songs like "Happy
Days Are Here Again," which became the Democratic
victory song of the FDR days, and "On the Sunny Side

of the Street." I like this song because it implies a reality of life: there are two sides of the street, and you can
choose on which one you want to walk! One is the
sunny side and the other the dark, cloudy side, and that
fact remains as true today as it was in the 1930s. Today,
as back then, we each have a choice on which side of life
we want to walk. The scripture commentator William
Barclay says that when you face the light, shadows fall
behind you. And when you turn your back on the light,
you stand in shadows. Those who live facing the light
live on the sunny side of life. Those whose backs are
turned away from the light, living oblivious to the luminous Divine Presence, live on the dark, shadowed side
of life. So if you wish to live in joy, live facing the Light.

Another great classic of that period was a song
about the most bizarre behavior any sane person can
imagine, "Singin' in the Rain." When it rains, people
quickly dash for cover, since only eccentrics or the
feeble-minded go out and dance and sing in a cloud-
burst. The rain in that song is a metaphor for misfortunes, for more often than not, when it rains, it pours!
The sparkling cheerfulness of this melody and lyrics
about singing and dancing in the rain is a prescription
for how to respond to the pains of life's troubles and
tribulations. When difficulties rain down on you, don't
sing a dirge; sing a happy song, and you find it isn't
raining anymore.

Another Depression-era lyric that uses the
metaphor of rain is, "Every time it rains, it rains pennies from heaven." The flowing melody and words of
"Pennies From Heaven" were an invitation to turn

upside down your attitude of despair to one of hope envisioned by turning upside down your umbrella to collect the shower of gifts falling from the heavens.

If you are not a singer, consider reciting as poetry Johnny Burke's lyrics to Arthur Johnston's music of this song:

> Every time it rains, it rains pennies from heaven.
> Don't you know each cloud contains pennies from heaven?
> You find your fortune falling all over town.
> Be sure to turn your umbrella upside down.
> Trade them for a package of sunshine and flowers.
> If you want the things you love,
> You must have showers . . .

I've stopped at this point in the song because the last two lines are so filled with truth they need their own space:

> If you want the things you love,
> you must have showers.

Even when logic tells us that life is a mixture of good days and bad, we live in the illusion that it is supposed to be all blue skies and sunshine. Life and love require showers, disappointments, setbacks, and dark days. For serious-minded, practical people this song asks a really silly question, "Don't you know each cloud contains pennies from heaven?" Yet when its poetic words are decoded, they contain an ancient truth: God loves us, and what appears as misfortune always contains pennies, small gifts, from heaven. As the song concludes, "So when you hear it thunder, don't run under a tree, there'll be pennies from heaven for you and me." When next the gloomy clouds gather overhead, or when it rains on your parade, hum, whistle, sing, or recite like poetry a few lines of the lyrics of this happy song. Even if you know only a few lines of the song, it holds magical power to somersault a bad day into a better one, and a tearful sad face into a smile of joy.

This reflection began with the advice of professional caregivers to sing songs to calm the anxieties of Alzheimer's patients with severe memory loss. The loss of happiness can also be a memory loss! Whenever some tribulation is permitted to grow to gargantuan size, it easily eclipses the memories of former good times. It erases memories of former times when difficulties were finally resolved in beneficial ways, when sicknesses were overcome, and the sun broke through the gray, overcast skies. The next time you find yourself down in the dumps, suffering from what could be called a "momentary" Alzheimer's attack, heal your blues by singing or even simply reciting the lyrics of a happy song.

fulfilling your
easter duty

Since 1215, Church law has prescribed that Catholics must, under pain of serious sin, perform their Easter duty. This consists of receiving Holy Communion during the Easter Season, the minimum of once a year. The Easter period for fulfilling this obligation was those weeks from the First Sunday of Lent to Trinity Sunday, eight weeks after Easter Sunday. To go to confession during this period, while not an absolute requirement, was also considered part of your Easter duty.

Is not the authentic Easter duty of all Christians, Protestant, Catholic, or Orthodox, to celebrate the resurrection by living joyously? Is not the true Easter duty also the will of God as Paul said in his letter to the Thessalonians? Laws such as the Church law of the

Easter duty, like any civil law, are the last resorts, the only option left when love fails to be the motivating force in life. Expressing your desire is another way of letting your will or intention be known. Does not the Beloved One desire that we live happy lives so we might abide constantly in the Joy of God?

Two thousand years have now passed since the human family learned that the Divine Beloved's desire was for all to live in joy! Practically speaking, no one expects the harshly competitive world of business and industry to be a joyful place. But sprinkled across the weary, workaday world are those exclusively set-aside zones of the sacred—places called church. Wouldn't it be a logical expectation based on scripture that these houses of God would also be houses of joy and shrines of happiness? They are indeed holy places of prayer and worship, yet how many of them resound with that jubilation contagious with happiness and hopeful optimism? Also, a spirit of cheerfulness regardless of the circumstance doesn't seem to be a defining mark of individual Christians. This lack of happiness may not be a religious but a sociological problem.

Gregg Easterbrook, in his *The Progress Paradox*, states an amazing fact: "The percentage of Americans who describe themselves as happy has not budged since the 1950s, though the typical person's real income has more than doubled!" He says many not only do not report being happier, they actually feel worse. Research conducted by Princeton University reveals that most people determine their happiness and wealth not by their present condition, but rather on whether they think their circumstances and income will improve in the coming years. Fifty years ago, the typical family had only one car, lived in a modest home, and few, if any, of their children attended college. Yet many people were cheerful, since they expected their standard of living to get better and better. The mood of this nation was high. Now since many, if not most, Americans no longer expect a better, more prosperous tomorrow, a pestering discontent festers in the nation. No longer do families believe that each year their lifestyle will improve, and parents today no longer expect that their children will have a higher standard of living than they have had.

Their best hope now is that with both spouses working they can manage to maintain their present standard of living. Many, unable to find happiness in the prospect of a better life and a higher salary, now seek to find it in an epidemic of shopping. This short-term happiness of consumerism is a national addiction after being bombarded by endless advertisements. This is also the reason Americans have the highest rate of debt in the world. Among all the industrialized nations of the world, we rank last in individual or family savings.

Americans and Europeans who have no hope that the coming years will bring them a better and higher standard of living therefore need to find a new gauge for happiness. Antiquated is that future-sighted telescope that held the promise of a higher standard of living, a larger home, and a better life in the coming years. What is needed today is not a telescope but a *here*scope: a viewing device to clearly see the present moment. By daily use of such an apparatus, they could see that they presently have all that is needed to be happy. A herescope produces contentment, and whenever you're satisfied, you are joyful.

If every home in the country, along with television and indoor plumbing, had a herescope, the potential consequences for the national economy would be absolutely devastating. All the malls in America would become ghost towns; millions upon millions working to manufacture all the "things" advertised on television would be unemployed. No need for alarm! Don't panic! So deeply ingrained in us is our red, white, and blue consumerism that most people even using a herescope daily would become sneaking, closet buyers. They would find clever ways to secretly feed their addiction, just as drinkers did during the old days of Prohibition. This ideal of contentment may not be possible for the multitude, but it is a possibility for those who wish to be happy and so choose to be satisfied with what they have. There are those who are content, have no need to buy anything to make them happier, and so are able to live in joy.

Easter is the great feast of happiness overflowing with joyous Alleluias. Easter is the great feast of joy, since it celebrates the promise of life victorious over death. And the Easter duty of every Christian isn't simply to be happy on Easter Sunday or even the fifty days after Easter, but all days. Belief in the resurrection of Jesus from the tomb, or in your own personal resurrection, is not enough to achieve the continuous living of a joyous life unless you practice contentment. Paradoxically, the best way to be assured of eternal happiness is by living in joy and contentment here and now since all death does is confirm *this* life for eternity.

seventeen

a **happy death**

The twentieth century's famous artist Pablo Picasso once said, "It takes a long time to become young again." Picasso labored a lifetime to capture in art the essence of his subjects with a primitive and childlike freedom. Most of us are socially conditioned to prefer artworks that resemble the realism of photographs, except for parents of small children.

My preschool-aged great-nephew Nathan gave me a drawing he made of Christ on the cross. This innocent's icon of the crucifixtion depicts a smiling Jesus! I've seen depictions of a laughing Jesus, which to be honest I did not care for, since they looked like toothpaste advertisements. Unlike those slick Hollywood-like images of a laughing, handsome Jesus, this icon by Nathan is haunting in a mystically disturbing way. It asks the question, "Did Jesus smile as he was dying?"

Crucifixion was the most painfully slow way to die, and so was reserved by the Romans and Persians for their most hideous of crimes—rebellion. Christians of today cannot fully comprehend how repulsively disgusting and shameful was the image of a crucified person. Because it was, in the early centuries, Jesus was never depicted dying on a cross! After the fourth century, images of Christ on the cross slowly began to appear, but he was depicted as serene, often as regal as a king, and never in painful agony. The image of Jesus dying in agony on the cross, so familiar today, would not appear for over a thousand years. While the Gospels report in detail his death agony, they also recorded his profound, unshakeable conviction that he and God were one. At the Last Supper, he told his disciples to rejoice for he was going back to the Father, to the source from which he had come. Since he told his disciples to rejoice in his death, did he experience joy in his dying?

Does my great-nephew Nathan's icon of Christ on the cross provide a profound meditation on how we are to die—with a smile? Doesn't fidelity to our call to rejoice always include doing so at our death? By what dispensation should death be excluded from living in joy? If, as we claim, death is the doorway to our complete and joyous unity with God, isn't at least a smile as we die a sign of our belief in that faith statement? To achieve this wondrous deathbed gift, practice is required. Practice makes perfect, and so practice smiling as you die in little bits and pieces: when incarcerated in a traffic jam, required to wait endlessly in a doctor's office, upon hearing some false scandalous gossip about yourself, accidentally losing hours of work on your computer, and any one of life's deadly array of difficulties. Practice, practice, and practice smiling, and you will develop the habit of a happy death.

A habit is a pattern of behavior that creates conduct requiring no thought or effort. Smiling in difficult times should be a holy habit, a term once used in Catholic religious orders for the unique, and usually centuries-old, style of clothing worn by monks and nuns. Religious habits identity those who wear them as members of a particular religious order or community. They also are symbolic of how the monk or nun has "put on Christ," and are intended to remind those who wear them daily of their religious vows of poverty, chastity, and obedience.

In early Christianity, the truly holy habits were not made of fabric; they were always rejoicing, praying ceaselessly, and giving thanks in all circumstances. Like the habits of religious orders, these also were forms of identification. When describing to pagans those who belonged to the new Christian movement, a second-century martyr by the name of Justin said, "We always give thanks!" If they were faithful to the admonition of Paul, along with their constant gratitude, they also were always prayerful and joyful. Jesus could have said, "By these habits will all know that you are my disciples."

d**o**n't delay joy

While writing the manuscript for this book I received a handmade card from an old friend, Joanne Callahan. She had made impressions on paper of autumn leaves and then colored them in stunning orange. Alongside the autumn leaves she had written in black ink, "Don't delay joy."

In the famous trinity of Thessalonians, Paul calls us to live in joy, prayer, and gratitude—whatever happens. To do this in our present world is extremely difficult, since the daily headlines overflow with the bad news of a disastrous war, the torture by our military of prisoners, governmental and corporate corruption, and with thousands losing their jobs, health care, and pensions. Instead of joy, aren't prophetic outrage and condemnation of those who are responsible for these evils a more appropriate or even required response from us? To confront evil with joyfulness instead of outrage feels like the cowardly complicity of silence. Cannot smiling instead of weeping only masquerade our impotency as individuals to change anything by denouncing social evils? These are distressing questions that challenge the validity of being happy and grateful in *all* circumstances, including those that are obliviously wicked. Of the three, only praying ceaselessly escapes censure, since nothing else seems possible.

Yet the world and humankind haven't changed significantly since Paul wrote to the Thessalonians. Wars of imperial aggression, exploitation of the weak and poor, along with governmental greed and corruption were not only as common as today—they were much worse. Yet early Christians living amid such evil, which for some included being slaves under the whip of callous masters, were called to do the will of God and live in joy, prayer, and gratitude. To live in joy is to abide in God who is love, and being an authentic prophet requires loving who and what you denounce. Prophets are God's spokespersons. To daily live with fidelity to those three virtues is acting prophetically, since they are nonviolent confrontations with evil.

The Master wasn't ambivalent when it came to anger, saying, "You shall not be angry." His life demonstrates clearly that those who live in God and engage in peaceful nonviolence will be victorious in the divine timetable of accountability. Those who live in patient, joyful confidence do so convinced that goodness will ultimately triumph over all evil. This rule of life does not exclude prophetic protest, only how it is expressed. Dissent in voice or symbolic action against the variety of

injustices of your church, local, state, or national government. The absence of dissent becomes silent agree-
ment to war, exploitation of the weak, neglect of the
poor, and discriminatory rules based on religious codes.

While your heart burns to exercise your prophetic
duty, exercise great care in how you fulfill this holy
office. Medical studies have shown that to become angry
with issues over which you have no power is unhealthy
for your body, especially your heart. Certainly anger is
harmful to your soul as well. Both Jesus and Buddha,
even lacking this medical and psychological knowledge,
forbid their disciples to be angry. So, be a prophet but a
non-angry, peaceful, and cheerful one.

Returning to Joanne's card about autumn-delayed
joy, I reflected that for ages the church's spirituality had
taught that we were to bear the heavy cross of injustices, oppression, and poverty in order to merit joy in
the next life of heaven. The negative spirituality of past
centuries saw the tribulations and miseries of this life as
sad consequences of both the sin of Adam and Eve and
one's own personal sins. In this spirituality, instead of
"Rejoice always," a more appropriate admonition
would have been "Be always gloomy." The sad plight of
the sin-cursed human family, even if they were baptized
into the risen Christ, was expressed in that popular
prayer "Hail, Holy Queen."

> To thee do we cry, poor banished children
> of Eve; to thee do we send up our sighs,
> mourning and weeping in this valley of tears.

This is no ancient prayer of ages past! In my lifetime it was prayed with great devotion. So if you were exiled from happiness, banished to dwell in the valley of tears, only the simple-minded would go about rejoicing and giving thanks. It is no wonder that there was so little joy in Christianity. For those living in prayer, gratitude, and joyfulness, a new, revised verse of the "Hail, Holy Queen" is needed, perhaps one such as this:

Hail, Happy Queen of Heaven,
to thee do we sing out our joyful praises,
we baptized, redeemed children of Eve,
your beloved sons and daughters in Christ.
To thee, Ever-joyful Mother, do we send up
our petitions, our joy, laughter, and smiles
in this world shimmering with the radiance
of your joyous love for your son and for us.

Today, be as cheerful as you can. Today—not tomorrow when your health is better or the world has a brief recess from wars and killing—rejoice. Today—not in heaven after you are dead—live in happiness and gratitude. Do not delay doing the will of God.

nineteen

living in joy

While today it is more commonly found in print than spoken, *"joie de vivre"* (pronounced jwah deh VEE-vruh) means literally "joy of living." This expression means more than contentment as it implies a zestful enthusiasm, a flamboyant joyfulness in just being alive. People with *joie de vivre* are able to find great enjoyment in every aspect of life. They find immense pleasure in both the new and the old, and by their enthusiastic enjoyment of ordinary things they magically transform the old into the new. Since they find such delight in going places and being in the company of others, their presence causes the world around them to glisten with luminosity. Because of their enjoyment of life, such people have magnetic personalities.

If any could be said to "rejoice always," it would have to be those possessing this ability to intensely enjoy life. When you recall that those living such attractively joyful lives are doing the will of God, as Paul said, then it is unfortunate that the first requirement for anyone to be canonized a saint isn't *joie de vivre*. Francis of Assisi, (whose nickname of "Frenchy" is the source of his name, Francis) stands out in that long line of solemn, if not sad-faced, saints as one who possessed *joie de vivre*. Francis's contagious cheerfulness in simply living was possible because he was possessed—not by the devil, but completely caught up and embraced by Divine Joy.

Typically in today's society, those who manifest *joie de vivre* are the very wealthy, since they have the money to enjoy every kind of luxury, fine wines, and gourmet foods. Their large bank accounts enable them to live carefree and leisurely lives, and they are often the sons and daughters of successful, hardworking, and driven millionaire businessmen whose lives of unrelenting diligence made the family fortune. Fate's ironic twist is that sadly these millionaires, because their work habits, are themselves unable to enjoy the taste of *joie de vivre*.

St. Francis, the patron of *joie de vivre*, proclaims loudly by his barefoot poverty that you don't need a fortune to live in joy. In fact, having a fortune may actually prevent it because wealth can cripple authentic joy. As the son of a rich merchant, he renounced his family fortune. His life illustrates the lesson that it isn't necessary to be a millionaire or billionaire, win the lottery, or inherit a fortune to live joyfully! What is needed, however, is an unconditional belief in the glad tidings of the Master that can so infatuate one as to become possessed by Divine Gladness. To this is added another requirement that may be even more difficult—

to intensely enjoy the material good things of life. What makes this so difficult is the need to swim upstream against the church's history of being highly suspicious of the pleasures of earthly life. In the medieval times of Francis of Assisi, this belief in the sinfulness of human pleasures was even far greater than it is today.

Traditional spiritual guides usually forbid or are highly suspect of the sensual delights of delicious food, fine wines, soul-stirring music, and the enchanting beauties of art, not to mention the exotic delights of human sexuality. Since the early ages of Christianity, these sensual delights have been judged to lead the devout believer astray, away from God and the rewards of the next life. In their place, fasting, abstinence, and celibacy were exalted as spiritual ideals. The monastic model of eating meager meals in silence, sleeping on hard beds, and living in bare, unadorned quarters remains for many the pattern out of which saints are cut. Rejoice today that instead of creation being cursed as evil by Eden's mistake, there is a new and healthier spirituality based on the original goodness of creation that also includes humankind. This wholesome outlook on nature, especially human nature, may finally permit Paul's vision of living in joy, gratitude, and prayer to be realized.

Old patterns of thought and behavior possess lingering echoes that can reverberate throughout life. So if you should feel that ancient religious shadow of suspicion slowly casting its long, dark silhouette of latent sin over your enjoyment of some pleasure in life—stop!

Then sing, hum, or whistle Jimmy McHugh's hit song of the 1930s Depression-era, "On the Sunny Side of the Street." If you're not a singer, then recite Dorothy Fields's lyrics to that song as an anti-gloom psalm.

Grab your coat, and get your hat.
Leave your worries on the doorstep.
Just direct your feet to the sunny side of the street.
Can't you hear a pitter-pat?
and that happy tune is your step.
Life can be so sweet
on the sunny side of the street.

Living happily as the song implies is a matter of choosing on which side of life you desire to walk. All streets have two sides! Everyone has worries—life without them is impossible—but you don't have to carry them around with you!

I used to walk in the shade
with those blues on parade . . .
but. . . . [I've] crossed over.
If I never have a cent,
I'll be rich as Rockefeller
gold dust at my feet,
on the sunny side of the street.

Marvelous is her line ". . . with those blues on parade," and quite insightful, since we can so easily parade our problems before others when we've chosen to live on the gloomy side of life. To cross over to the sunny side to enjoy life doesn't require great wealth, since those who possess *joie de vivre* are indeed, as Dorothy Fields's words say, richer than any Rockefeller billionaire. As usual in God's divine comedy of life, there is a paradoxical reality that to possess *joie de vivre* only requires being possessed by joy eternal. Possession is occupation, and the first requirement of being occupied is to move out!

I, who long to be alive in your joyfulness,
know that to be filled to overflowing with You
requires that I drain my cup of gleeless joys,
the sludge of promised, purchased delights
that the world constantly pours into my cup.

Empty me of me; drain me out dry,
and so with illusion emptied and hollowed
then You can fill me with the enduring
joys of meals with those I love,
and leisure times spent in creation
and with You.

twenty

does suffering bring out the **best** or the **worst** in you?

In a disaster, as some people heroically rush to the scene to assist those who are in need, others use the chaotic situation to loot stores and homes. These kinds of opposite human responses are the source of the common expression "disaster brings out the best and the worst in people." And what is true for large calamities seems true for minor, personal ones. When confronted with sickness, or some physical or emotional suffering, some remain cheerful as they silently tackle their afflictions. Others react to their suffering by being irritable, grouchy, surly, and impatient. We can now rephrase the saying about the two responses to a disaster, "Sickness brings out the best and the worst in people!"

Ageless wisdom tested by time shouldn't be contested, yet is that old adage really true that tribulations bring out the best or worst in you? The answer, it seems, is that they bring out only what is already in you! If you are striving to live as happily as you can, regardless of what fate drops at your door, you can greet it with confident optimism because you believe that whatever it is can be resolved in a beneficial way. An outburst of violent anger at some minor misfortune is more than a reaction; it is often an eruption of subterranean anger and hostility. Similarly, a smiling acceptance of the same misfortune is but the bubbling up to the surface of a hidden spring of inner joyfulness. Living a cheerful life, then, is but the result of abiding as consciously as is possible with the hidden inner presence of the Divine Mystery. So the next time you are visited by some unexpected misfortune, let your response be for you a signal of your care for your abiding Divine Guest, or your neglect of that guest. If you respond in anger or despair, let it be an alarm to awaken you to your negligent hospitality to your guest.

I first came across the image of "the Guest" for the divine presence in the writings of the fifteenth-century Indian spiritual master Kabir. In his love poems/psalms, he was fond of referring to the divine presence as "the Guest." In one of them he says, "Hope to find the Guest while you are alive, leap into that experience . . . what you call 'salvation' belongs only to those who are living." In that same one, Kabir concludes with wisdom about being overly attentive to the methods of meditation and spiritual practices: "When you are earnestly searching for the Guest, it is passionate love and intensity of your longing for the Guest that actually accomplishes the work." In another he says, "The Guest is inside you, and also within me; just as a sprout is hidden inside a seed . . . the arrogance of reason has severed us from that love . . . let your arrogance go, and look inside. I love the Guest that is inside of me."

When we look inside with faith we realize that the Guest, the beloved, dwells perpetually within and saturates our every fiber and atom. While we cannot usually anticipate some unexpected difficulty or disappointment, we can attend to the rituals of hospitality. In the ancient world, strangers and visitors at your door were treated with great respect, since it was believed the gods made their visitations disguised as strangers. The ability to respond positively with a smile in all circumstances requires careful observance of the first of the ancient sacraments—the ritual of hospitality. A good host or hostess doesn't ignore the presence of a distinguished guest in the home but is eager to visit and to care for his or her every need. Hospitality requires that you don't busy yourself with the normal household duties oblivious to the presence of your guest. And when duties actually do require your attention, you remain constantly mindful of the presence of your guest. So, come hell or high water, despite how dark and dismal the circumstances, you will be surprised at how easy it is to respond to them with joy and optimism if you practice the ancient art of hospitality.

twenty-one

"hurrah!"a joyous shout of **"God is here!"**

Some believe that the word *hurrah*—that raucous shout of joyful jubilation heard at times of touchdowns and thrilling victories—comes from the Slavonic word for paradise, *hu-raj*. While some say otherwise, I say let scholars quibble! I find that old Slavonic word source to be mystically correct. Whenever we are caught up in euphoric jubilation, are we not in paradise, enjoying the company of God? Untamed joy is euphoric; it is ecstatic, taking us out of ourselves and into God.

Paradise is the symbolic place of all innocent pleasures since it is pre-sin, if you adhere to the Eden story as history. Being pre-sin, paradise is also pre-religion, so you will never hear in public worship this wild shout of joy at the zenith moment of the ritual. The absence of

wild delight inside the sacred space of churches and
during worship times seems to imply that you must
look for paradise elsewhere on earth.

Religion is respectable. At least it strives mightily to
imitate the Almighty, whom it deems divinely somber
like an emperor on his throne. Is the unbreakable rule
that when in church "one must be silent, somber, and
solemn; babies are not to cry; and no one is to laugh" a
contrivance of religion's clerical caretakers since they
fear they are not taken seriously by a majority of the
population? Does this fear find validity in the old adage
"except for funerals and weddings, religion is only for
women and children"? Is our western Christianity's joy-
less, somber Puritan heritage the source of our solemn
religious reverence? Or is it because religion is the rigid
backbone of the bourgeois middle class who themselves are preoccupied with respectability?

Whether for religious or sociological reasons,
churches, like public libraries, are certainly not the
places for uninhibited jubilation. So if you want to
enjoy primitive paradise prayer and be ecstatic in your
praise of God, pray alone in your room or out in the
wilderness. Also, instead of your usual response,
"Thank God," the next time something truly wonderful happens to you, consider an alternative and be auda-
ciously joyful by shouting out "hurrah!" Translation:
"I'm with God in Paradise!"

Hallelujah, the pious cousin of *hurrah*, is a joyous
exclamation of praise that unfortunately today is usually associated only with black spirituals and Pentecostal
worship. This exultant cry of "Hallelujah!" has a history almost as ancient as old Methuselah (said to have

lived for 969 years) and is Hebrew for "Praise Yahweh!"
It was originally a directive for a temple singer before
the communal recitation of certain psalms and as a
final proclamation by all the worshipers at the conclusion of some other psalms. When the Hebrew
Scriptures were translated into Greek, *hallelujah*
became *allelouia*. In Medieval Latin this was *alleluja*,
which then of course became our contemporary
alleluia. Interestingly, out of reverence for the popular
use of both of these in the apostolic church, these
words have never been translated. Both *alleluia* and *hallelujah* have the strength to stand on their own feet, and
remain as vibrantly enthralling as they were two thousand or more years ago.

Alleluia was used by early Christians as a prayer-
word and was also chanted as a work song. In the early
fifth century, St. Jerome reported that farmers chanted
it as they toiled in their fields, and sailors sang it as a
rowing song. Mothers taught this word of joy to their
children as their first spoken word, and Roman soldiers
battling barbarians used it as their battle cry and war
song. This habitual use by early Christians of the joyous *Alleluia* as a chant to accompany their labors
implies a desire to live joyful lives. In its public worship,
the Church first reserved the *Alleluia* as a victorious cry
of rejoicing only for the fifty days of Eastertide, at
funerals, and at burials. Gradually its use spread to the
rest of the year, except for the season of Lent.

An interesting bit of medieval lore is the *depositio*,
or funeral and burial of the *Alleluia* that occurred
before the beginning of Lent. The Western Church,
considering joy and penance as contradictory, banned

the use of the *Alleluia* in public worship from the third Sunday before Lent until Easter Sunday. The Lenten penitential season was a time of fasting, not only from food, but also from expressions of happiness, so the *Alleluia* was eliminated from public worship. This church regulation occasioned local customs of the funeral and burial of the *Alleluia*, accompanied by weeping and moaning. Whether or not the common people continued to chant it as a work song and mothers continued to teach it to their infants during Lent isn't recorded. Perhaps they did continue using it. The Greek Orthodox Church didn't discontinue using it in its Lenten worship. In that orthodox tradition, it is a lesson for us.

The majority of churchgoers today most likely do not even notice the absence of the *Alleluia* during the Sundays of Lent! In our contemporary society, this ancient sound of joy is also no longer chanted as a work song. In fact, it sometimes seems that joy itself is dead and buried. Let us be inspired by the brothers and sisters of the Greek Orthodox churches and continue to use the ancient, rich joy prayer of the *Alleluia* regardless of how penitential our lives may have become. So if daily cares or frustrations with your church or the government, or an irritating coworker have caused you to bury your joy, go out and dig it up! Go to its tomb, and boldly call it back to life as the Master did with the dead and buried Lazarus while his family and friends joyously shouted, "Hallelujah! Hurrah—God is here!"

twenty-two

joy o' the mountains

"Joy o' the Mountains" is the folk name given to a trailing arbutus plant found in the mountains of the American South. This creeping plant with clusters of pinkish or white flowers is among the most fragrant of all wildflowers. This trailing evergreen plant with beautiful, fragrant blossoms is almost impossible to grow in cultivated home flower gardens, yet it thrives in the wild!

The spontaneous *hallelujah* or *hurrah* of the last reflection, like the plant "Joy o' the Mountains," is also not found in sophisticated society or in flower garden parties. Wild joy is wisely kept under lock and key until one is far away from somber, sensible people since they would judge it as the expression of a fool, or worse—the mad. The Master, like that most fragrant of wildflowers of the South, also preferred the wild places to the sophisticated gatherings of the elite. He was known to frequently disappear to climb the mountains and be alone in the wilderness where his disciples said he went to pray.

In his book *Orthodoxy*, British author G. K. Chesterton states that the gospels show us a Jesus who, since he was fully human, expresses every human emotion. He is reported to have been sad, tired, and hungry; to have wept at the tomb of his dead friend Lazarus; to have become extremely angry in the temple; and to have suffered the agonizing pains in his passion. However, Chesterton says that there is one human emotion that he is never reported to have expressed—his joy! The gospels contain not a single report of Jesus' ever laughing or even smiling. Since these are significant signs of being human, Chesterton conjectures the reason Jesus never expressed any joy was because he knew he had to keep it hidden. Unlike his other human emotions, his sense of humor was so saturated with divine hilarity that he felt it had to be concealed from mortals.

Chesterton says that because this was the case, Jesus went off alone up into the mountains so that in solitude he could be overwhelmed with laughter. Not ordinary laughter, but rather a divinely wild, rollicking laughter at the foolishness of his beloved disciples, who couldn't grasp the meaning of his parables. That they weren't able to decode God's madness in his teaching didn't produce in him sadness and disappointment, but wild divine hilarity. So rather than Savior or Redeemer, the folk name of that attractive southern plant, "Joy o' the Mountains," is a better name for Jesus.

An adaptation of "Joy to the World," the Christmas carol theme song of this book, could be "The Joy o' the Mountains Has Come!"

twenty-three

complain always, and in all circumstances

Nowhere in the Bible will you find the admonition "Complain always and in all circumstances!" But you would think it was a biblical injunction or one of the Ten Commandments since so many people seem to be constantly complaining about something. These complainers find fault with the weather, today's high prices, taxes, the lax morals, the decline of church attendance by young people, noisy obnoxious neighbors, the great influx of foreign immigrants, the corruption of government officials. . . . Ah, the complainer's mournful litany is endless!

"To whine always" is the household version of "always complain." This vice takes the form of grumbling about countless small things that happen around the house or the behaviors of certain family members. Small children whine, incessantly pestering their parents for something they want. Adults also whine, only they do so in a more sophisticated style. If you have developed a life pattern of complaining and whining about everything under the sun, it will then be nearly impossible for you "to rejoice always and be grateful regardless of the circumstances." While "all things are possible with God," even the Almighty is handicapped by entrenched habits that enslave us. One can easily become a slave complainer!

Yet who willingly enters into slavery of human bondage, even if it is only that of constant grumbling? Naturally, no one knowingly does! African peoples more than a century and a half ago were captured by slave dealers or caught unaware by their own tribe and sold into slavery. Slavery continues to exist in the world today, and the people most commonly enslaved today have not been captured, but rather captivated. They have been slowly lured by the pleasure rewards of illegal drugs, alcohol, or consumerism into the slavery of addiction. The same is true with whiners who get hooked on whining's rewards.

Complainers get attention. They also frequently get their way, and whining children learn this lesson early in life. Complainers become addicted to grumbling since one of their pleasure rewards is to have others feel sorry for them, to pity them for the tribulations that God or fate has dealt them. Don't feel sorry for your whining neighbors or friends! However, do feel pity for them—just as you would for heroin addicts—since they also have caged themselves in a living hell. But isn't existence on earth intended to be a living hell since, by Adam's sin, humanity was banished from the happiness of Paradise? If life post-Adam is supposed to be hell, then complaining and lamenting are only normal human behaviors, and they could also be valid expressions of prayer!

Among the seventy-some books of the Bible, one is exclusively for prayers of complaining: the Book of Lamentations. Written by an unknown author once thought to be the prophet Jeremiah, these poems of misery were written nearly six hundred years before the time of Jesus. These religious authors give mournful voice to human suffering, misfortune, and profound grief in dirgelike poetry. The author-lamenter complains directly to the Almighty about God's neglectful absence, "you have wrapped yourself with a cloud so that no prayer can pass through."[1] He continues to bewail the pitiable state of the people.

> We are weary, we are given no rest . . .
> Our skin is black as an oven from the
> scorching heat of famine.
> The joy of our hearts has ceased . . .
> our hearts are sick . . .
> Why have you forgotten us completely?
> Why have you forsaken us these many days?[2]

His litany of complaints concludes in despair, "you have utterly rejected us, and are angry with us beyond measure."[3]

So unique in all the pages of the Bible is the New Testament's imperative "rejoice always," not simply at times of a bountiful harvest, some victory over one's enemies, or at a wedding feast—but always! What one does find in the Jewish-Christian scriptures instead of joyfulness or gleeful gratitude are complaining and grumbling to God about all the sufferings and ruthless realities of life. These sad laments are not confined to the Book of Lamentations, since more than one-third of the psalms are also woeful lamentations. An example of such woeful wailing is Psalm 41, where the psalmist groans,

> My enemies speak evil of me . . .
> and if one of them comes to visit me,
> he does not speak sincerely;
> his heart stores up malice,
> he goes out and then talks.
> All who hate me whisper together
> against me; evil things they plan
> against me: "A deadly disease has got
> hold of him," and "he who lies there will
> not rise again." Even my friend, in
> whom I trusted, who ate my bread,
> lifted his heel against me.

These mournful, psalm-prayer complaints are not addressed to the wind, but spoken directly to God, and they ask that painful, unanswerable question, "Why have I been singled out for such misery? Tell me why must I, your faithful steward, be so sadly afflicted." So,

if you're a chronic complainer, it seems you have biblical justification for your griping and grumbling, and not
simply to family and friends. So, in your prayers, why
shouldn't you also feel free to complain to God and
to bombard heaven with your grievances? But what
about Paul's insistence that we are to rejoice always—
an "always" that seems to cover all circumstances and
situations?

[1] Lamentations 3:43
[2] Lamentations 5:5–20
[3] Lamentations 5:22

grumpy prayers
lead to canticles of joy

By making the Hebrew psalms the core of its official daily prayers, the Church seems to offer
them as models for our personal prayers. Since a
third of these psalms are woeful lamentations and sad
songs of unhappiness, why shouldn't one out of three
of our personal prayers also be tear-soaked laments?
Most people believe that God rules the universe. If this
is so, then God is ultimately responsible for all that happens on earth, including natural and personal disasters.
Even if this belief is difficult to accept, it does seem
that somehow or other God must be responsible for
what goes wrong. So why not consider complaining to
God about what is wrong in your life? The following
two criticizing psalm-prayers are examples or models
for your complainer prayer:

The Cancer Victim Psalm

Why have you abandoned me to the misery
of nauseating rages of chemotherapy?
My hair has fallen out; my family shuns me
being a laughingstock to all; I hate to go out.
As Jesus told us, I prayed with faith to you
to be spared this curse of cancer: were you deaf?

Are you not God, and present everywhere?
Where were you when I cried aloud to you?
Were you at the farthest edge of the cosmos,
creating a new better world, one free of cancer,
AIDS, starvation, wars, and poverty

and so too busy to heed my pleas for your help?

O God, why have you cursed me with this cancer,
abandoning me to the grave and a horrible death?

A Lamentation for a Lost Job

Your son Jesus promised if we sought your
    Kingdom
with all our hearts, all we needed would be given us!
Well I've done that! I've dutifully gone to church,
believed in you, trusted in your providential care!
Now look at me, I've lost my job, my livelihood.
My neighbor, a devout atheist, never worships you,
yet he has a big, fat pension that yearly allows him

to winter for three months in sunny, warm Arizona!
Tell me God, do you love him more than me to cast
this loyal servant into the hell of the unemployed?

God, I'm out of work! Have you forgotten
I've got monthly house and car payments
and children to feed?
With zero savings, I'm on the precipice of poverty.
Where will I ever get the money to buy groceries
for my family, pay my mortgage and medical bills?

Jesus promised that if we prayed to you with faith,
all we needed would be given to us—I need a job!
Jesus said that you grieve for every little sparrow
that falls to the earth, so God, what about me who
has fallen upon hard times, do you grieve for me?

With Jesus on the cross I pray, 'My God,
my God, why have you forsaken me?'

Most Christians plunged into some personal catastrophe or suffering would find it extremely uncomfort-
able to pray imitating either of these prayers.
Complaining to God seems insulting, since who are we
to complain directly to God about divine absenteeism
and bureaucratic delays in the answering of our
prayers? Instead of being cranky with God when
misfortune comes, Christians are expected to surrender
to their fate and pray with tearful acceptance, "Thy will
be done!" However, the next time you are visited by
some dire tribulation, seriously consider saying your
own grumbling prayers because of their great value.

Bellyaching prayers to God are the mourning melody of
the overture to the prayers of rejoicing and giving
thanks. They are also prayers of the Spirit since they are
not hiding from reality.

Walter Brueggemann, the distinguished Old
Testament scholar, says that the prophets and poets of
Israel did not live in unreality and were not pious
romantics. Rather, he said that their prayers embrace all
of life, its delights and its sadness, its wedding dances
and funeral wakes, times of anger and bitter anguish.
Brueggemann believes that, unlike those of Israel, our
Christian public worship and personal prayers suffer
because they fail to address the anguish of modern
urban loneliness and the other harsh realities of life. An
example of this exclusion from our worship of life's
painful realities is evident in our funeral and burial
liturgies. These now are void of poignant prayers of
lamenting over the loss of a loved one. Clerical creators
of the funeral rites have excluded from them the human
torment of agonized mourning, that tear-soaked sadness we all feel at the death of a loved one. They apparently believe that this contradicts the Easter belief of
the resurrection. As a result, those very human expressions of sobbing and wailing cannot be ritualized in our
funeral services. They are treated as if they were hereti-
cal expressions, signs of disbelief. It is not psychologi-
cally or spiritually healthy in either communal or
personal prayer to exclude the painful dimensions of
our lives, or to suppress our natural doubts about
God's fidelity, even God's existence.

Brueggemann wisely observes that those woeful Hebrew psalms and lamentations are addressed to someone—God! When our sufferings and conflicts are made part of the raw material of our prayers, we begin the critical task of resolving them by working with God to creatively heal them. When we are brutally honest in prayer, expressing our anger and disappointment with God, instead of being polite and deferential, then the Compassionate One can be actively engaged with us in truly transforming ways. Brueggemann maintains that because the prayers of Israel were both honest and a dialogue, they were able to produce joy.

Patricia Datchuck Sánchez, in one of her articles in the publication *Celebration*, quotes a newspaper story from Budapest apparently written in the days of the old Communist regime. A man walks into a police station seeking the necessary documents of permission for him to emigrate to Western Europe. "Aren't you happy here?" asked the official. "I have no complaints," answered the Hungarian. "Are you dissatisfied with your work?" Again he answered, "I have no complaints." "Are you, then, perhaps discontented with your living conditions?" "I have no complaints about them." Exasperated the official asked, "Then, why do you want to go the West?" "Because," the man said, "there I can have complaints!"

This story illustrates the necessity of having the freedom to speak your mind to God, to complain about your miseries without fear of reprisals. Apparently Israelites of old felt that their uniquely intimate relationship with God freed them to honestly and openly speak their minds. Surely this marvelous liberty to gripe or give glory to God isn't only a prerogative of the Jews. If anything, Christians—if they truly believe the teachings of the Master—have an even more intimate relationship with God and so should feel a greater freedom to complain. So even if your pastor or spiritual director says the opposite, don't be afraid to grumble loudly to God. You may be surprised to find that by so doing you can begin to honestly rejoice—even in the midst of your suffering. Since your religious tradition and prayer books lack griping prayers, feel both free and creative to compose your own since they will usher you into joyful praise.

This reflection concludes by revisiting the Cancer Victim Psalm as it might be prayed by someone striving to live joyfully—regardless of the circumstances.

The Cheerful Cancer Victim Psalm

While I hate the nauseating rages of my chemo,
I rejoice in the gift of this healing medicine
since in the world only a few can receive it.
My bald head that so embarrasses me also
reminds me of the head of a newborn babe.

I see it as a gift of a second chance in life,
of being reborn to live life with more zest,
to love more, and enjoy life more intensely.
While I rejoice that my hair will soon grow back,
I pray my old, robotic way of living will not.

I prayed it wasn't cancer, and you seemed deaf!
But you weren't! You were working through
my medicines and doctors healing my sickness.
My soul joyfully magnifies you, my Holy Healer,
for you have done great things for me. Thank you!

clinging to the **faith** doggedly but without joy

Evelyn Waugh, the popular British author of books like *Brideshead Revisited* and *The Loved One*, was raised as an Anglican. Having been pious as a youth, he had considered entering the Anglican priesthood. In 1930, at the age of twenty-seven, he had a conversion experience and became a Roman Catholic. He later said that this conversion experience and his Catholic spirituality were central in his writing. Waugh wrote about people and their struggles to believe in God in a world where the sense of the sacred seemed to be evaporating like the morning fog.

As a convert he had been attracted to the ritualized Roman Mass and all the other medieval trappings of the Church. So he found the reforms of the Second Vatican Council in the 1960s, with the Mass no longer in Latin, to be a calamity. He wrote, "I cling to the faith doggedly but without joy."

The reforms of that council ushered in a vibrant new age of change that was dynamically alive in Spirit. But, as the prophet Jesus predicted, new wine can't be poured into old wineskins. Waugh was one of those of whom he said, "People prefer the old wine to the new wine." The restorative papacy of John Paul II and the old wine lovers of the Vatican slowly and definitely began the return of those old rituals, devotions, and the clerical climate of former times. If Waugh were alive today, he would be rejoicing to see the return of that which he so loved about the "old" Catholic Church. Paradoxically, his words about "clinging without joy to the faith" can be a valid motto for the large numbers of faithful who today sadly lament the restoration of the clerical culture and the practices of the pre-Vatican Council Church. If you are tempted to use Evelyn Waugh's words, "I cling doggedly to my faith, but without joy," don't!

Indeed, cling doggedly, even tenaciously, to your faith—but do so joyfully. Never allow any pronouncements of the papacy and the hierarchy—or even local edicts issued by those little popes who stand in parish pulpits—to steal your delight in life. Don't bother to write letters to Rome—complain directly to God!

The previous chapter encouraged prayers of grumbling, so don't hesitate to knock loudly on God's door and complain about what's gone wrong in your church. Pray with faith, and I'll wager you will hear something like this:

Ah, you sound just like my son Jesus! How he used to lament to me, moaning over the wretched worship of temple and its priesthood or the hypocrisy of the village elders with their strict observance of the petty religious rules. So, I would remind him that at his birth the angels sang, "Joy to the world! The Lord is come!" And I would remind him that the title "Lord" meant a savior, a rescuer. "So son," I would say to him, "be the Joy of the world! Become the joyful rescuer of religion. Liberate it from those priests and those rigidly correct temple rituals. Make love your greatest commandment, not obedience to rituals or moral codes! And son—like opening a lark's birdcage—set me free! Rescue me from the temple tabernacle so I can accompany you into the marketplace, to work alongside you as you labor in your woodshop and in your loving of those whom society finds the most unlovable. I can love them. Son, don't be sad. When those frowning, pious, gloom peddlers of guilt challenge you about not observing some minuscule religious law, instead of groaning inwardly, just smile and laugh. And son, whenever you laugh, remember that you are in the Holy of Holies in my presence, for I am Joy Eternal! When those elders or priests question you, don't worry about how to answer them, for I'll put the words on your lips. Even better, I give you the best of all arguments—smiling silence!"

faith to **remove mountains** and moaning

To rejoice always and in all circumstances is possible—if you have faith. Don't let that condition frighten you, since you don't need an enormous amount of faith. As the Master was fond of telling his disciples, just a pinch will do. "If you have faith the size of a mustard seed, you will say to this mountain, 'Move from here to there,' and it will move; and nothing will be impossible for you."[1] Just a pinch of trusting God has the explosive power to easily remove both a mountain and moaning—the groaning of sadness. Few, if any, have need to remove a mountain, but many of us need to remove melancholy. So be glad-hearted that living a happy life is possible, since nothing is impossible for those with faith.

An example of such powerful faith is found in the writings of John Henry Newman (1801–1890), a British scholar and an Anglican convert to Catholicism who eventually became a cardinal of the Church. In his book *Apologia pro Vita Sua*, Newman wrote of his life, religious conversion, and profound conviction of God's presence in his life. He believed that God had created him to do some definite service, committed him to a particular work not given to another. He wrote that because of his trust in God, if he were sick, somehow his illness would serve God since he believed deeply that God does nothing in vain. He said he would remain steadfast in his faith even if God removed all his friends and made him sadly afflicted of soul. By his profound trusting of God, Newman provides us with an example of relying upon the providence of God that whatever happens will in some mysterious way serve a divine purpose. So whatever your difficulties—sickness, desertion by friends, or a hopeless sense of desolation—trust that in some unexplainable way they will serve God's ends and lead you to calm and confident joy. This quiet joy that flows from simply being embraced by God isn't pretending your misfortune doesn't exist. It is, rather, a silent granite boulder to which you can cling in the face of the howling winds of sadness that threaten to sweep you away into hell. This faith—more correctly a profound trust in the incomprehensible Divine Mystery—requires a companion. This is especially so for Americans and other industrialized people. Surprisingly, this crucial necessity is found in exploring the very opposite of happiness—sadness!

In the evolution of the word *sad* is found a clue to living a joyous life. The old Indo-European root of *sad* originally meant "to satisfy," coming from *satis*, Latin for "sufficient." By medieval times *sad* had taken on the meaning of "solid or dense," and when attributed to someone it meant he or she was a serious person. By the sixteenth and seventeenth centuries its meaning changed again and was applied to metal products such as *sad-iron* and also, surprisingly, to bread! The expression *sad-bread* meant "a loaf of bread that has not yet risen." What once denoted something solid slowly evolved into meaning "serious or grave," and then finally was used exclusively for "unhappy or sorrowful." The clue to the necessary companion of faith, needed to live a happy life, is contained in the history of the word *sad*.

If you haven't found that clue yet, reread the sentence about seventeenth-century *sad-bread* for dough that hadn't risen. Today 99 percent of us buy our bread in a store already baked, and so we need a brief review of bread baking. After the ingredients of flour, water, and yeast have been mixed into dough, it is placed into a baking pan. The next ingredient is time, which is necessary for the dough to rise. Kept at a temperature of around ninety-eight degrees Fahrenheit, the dough slowly rises until it is no longer sad-bread. Then it's placed in the oven and baked. If you find it difficult being happy because you are enduring a particularly sad time in your life, remember the key ingredients for making bread—time and temperature. The Master used the metaphor of bread baking for the appearance of the

Kingdom of God, saying that it required a pinch of yeast. He could have added that patience is also needed to give the sad-bread time to rise. If your intention is to try to live a joyful life, then the warmth of your passionate, loving God must be married to patient waiting. Having to wait isn't easy for us since we're not a patient people! Spoiled by the instant communication of cell phones, television, rapid microwave cooking, and instant-drying paint, we have lost or never learned the art of patient waiting.

Those technological marvels also steal our happiness since they inflect us with impatience. Being impatient is to be irritated, annoyed. To remain pleasant or cheerful while enduring a prolonged personal or family difficulty requires persistent patience along with faith-filled prayer! God's creative resolutions aren't instantaneous. So as you suffer the pains of waiting, don't pretend to be happy. Don't force being joyful. Quiet patience leads to quiet joy if you can place your trust in the truthfulness of Paul's inspired words, "We know that all things work together for good for those who love God."[2] To "know" (have knowledge of) that infallible process of creative transformation means living in hope and trusting in God, who always brings goodness out of evil and joy out of sadness. This conversion, like bread baking, takes time. So be always patient and always trusting and always joyful.

[1] Matthew 17:20
[2] Romans 8:28

rejoice always
but also **mourn**

The only way to avoid witnessing the appalling sufferings, massive starvation, and pitiable plight of millions upon millions of people in the world is by not watching television. The human heart, having not evolved along with today's technology, numbs itself to the pain to prevent being crushed by these horrible visions of horrendous suffering. It is customary for the news reporter of an airliner crash in a foreign land to say, "Three hundred people died in the crash, but there were no Americans on board." This news policy challenges us to ask ourselves, "If Americans were among the dead, would we be more inclined to bemoan this tragic disaster?" We do not mourn for those we see in such misery on television because we have not yet evolved to a comprehensive compassion that is divinely global. Yet when we numb ourselves to the painful sorrows of those half a world away, we do so at our own risk since we simultaneously prevent ourselves from soul-stirring joys. Divorce yourself from feeling one emotion and you concurrently destroy your ability to enjoy its opposite, companion emotion. Engaging in suffering seems second nature to Christians since they are called to imitate Jesus, whose most prevailing image is suffering on the cross.

Oscar Wilde once commented, "It is rarely in the world's history that its ideal has been one of joy. The worship of pain has far more often dominated the world." The cult of the martyrs in both Christianity and Islam could be used to illustrate Wilde's point. In both these religions sainthood is the glorious reward for those dying painfully for their faith. Halos are rarely, if ever, bestowed on those who live a long, joyous life, since living happily isn't always recognized as a religious ideal. Silent endurance of any physical pain and suffering is an ideal regularly held up for imitation. Forgetting your own safety to rescue another in distress, or dying for your country and its flag, are considered by society its highest ideals. As Wilde observed, worship or admiration of pain endured for noble causes has dominated the values of the world, not living in joy.

For centuries Christians were taught to endure the sadness of an unhappy marriage, the misery of dreadful working conditions, or being crippled at birth as God's will. The admonition was to suffer now in this vale of tears so you can rejoice in the next life. The saintly Charles de Foucauld expressed his conventional

Christian concept of not expecting happiness in this life
since joy was reserved for the next, when in 1897 he
wrote this meditation to God:

> You tell me that I will be happy with the blessed
> happiness of the last day...that as miserable as I am,
> I am like a palm tree planted beside living water. . . .
> That in due season I will bear fruit . . . when the time
> is right. And when will this time be? For each one,
> this time will be at the Judgment. . . .

Kabir, the fifteenth-century Indian poet-mystic, who
was quoted in an earlier reflection, challenged such theology of delayed joy, a spirituality that is still preached
today:

> Jump into experience while you are alive!
> The idea that the soul will join with the
> ecstatic, just because the body is rotten
> —is all fantasy.
> What is found now is found then.
> Make love now with the divine
> and in the next life you will
> have the face of satisfied desire. . . .

The Master encouraged his disciples to find the
buried hidden treasure, the pearl of great price, not in
the next life but in this life. He also reminded his
disciples to find happiness in the misfortunes of life
when he named those whom God esteemed as blessed
in his Beatitudes. In their number he did not include
the wealthy, famous, and powerful who are usually

considered the most fortunate and so the happiest. He declared blessed, honorable, and happy are those who mourn, for they shall be comforted. Did he mean that their mourning would be changed now, or in the next life, or was he implying that those who know the depths of the sea of sorrow are capable of tasting overflowing joy?

We usually consider this Beatitude about those who mourn as addressed to those who grieve at the death of a dearly loved family member or friend or are suffering some grave injustice. Is it possible that he invites all, even those whose lives are not sorrowful, to become blessedly happy by embracing the sorrows of others and so being able to mourn with them? This would require not the radical surgery of a heart transplant, but a heart stretch! In this mystical procedure no anesthesia is given: the Spirit pushes outward on the walls of the heart until it is big enough to hold the sorrows of the world. The Master's unconventional litany declares God's canonization process. It is those who mourn, who hunger for justice; it is the poor, the single-minded of heart, the merciful, and the peacemakers who are the blessed. They are the saints. Unlike the Church's canonization process, God's route to holiness requires no healing miracles, lifelong celibacy, or membership in a religious order, or even in the Catholic Church! Jesus would say, "Seek not to be canonized!" Rather, then, seek to be counted among those fortunate, happy, and blessed whom the Master promised would be consoled and rejoice greatly here and in heaven, where their reward would be the greatest. Seek also to be gifted by the Spirit of equilibrium with the ability to perform that divinely acrobatic balancing act of mourning while also rejoicing.

dwell in
j°yfulness

The Master noticed that two men who happened to be disciples of John the Baptist were following him. He asked them, "What are you looking for?" "Rabbi, where are you staying?" they answered. "Come and see," he said to them, and they came and stayed in his humble peasant lodgings.[1] The gospel writer says that the hour was near sunset, which is symbolic since it can be connected to other sunset accounts: the sunset Seder meal and the sunset meal of Emmaus. At the sunset Last Supper on the night before his death, Jesus gifted his disciples "that my joy may be in you, and that your joy may be complete."[2] Aware of their anguish as he spoke of his approaching death, he promised, "but I will see you again, and your hearts will rejoice, and no one will take your joy from you."[3] Then at sunset on the day of his resurrection, two of his disciples on the road met a stranger and invited him to share supper with them at the village of Emmaus. As they broke bread, they realized that the stranger was really their beloved and now risen Master. Of his presence they said, "Were not our hearts burning within us while he was talking to us on the road, while he was opening the scriptures to us?"[4]

"Hearts on fire" beautifully describes the condition of intense joy and love. Is it not possible that those two disciples of John the Baptist who spent the night with Jesus also had an Emmaus-like experience? Did not their hearts burst into flames when they experienced that he resided in radiant happiness, not a Palestinian peasant's hut? So captivated were they that the next day Andrew, who was one of the two, raced home to bring his brother Simon Peter back to Jesus so he could also become his disciple.

The Gospels are mute about this magnetic, joyous spirit of the Master. It is not my intent to piously read this dynamic quality into his life story, but the gospel writers leave out more than they included in their story of Jesus. I am convinced that, recorded or not, his magnetic, joyous spirit explains his charisma that attracted disciples and large crowds, even small children. By nature, small children are not usually attracted to the typical stern religious personalities. While politicians and religious personalities reach out to pick up babies and pat little children on the head, they—not the children—initiate this physical contact. Yet in the

Gospels, children clustered around Jesus, even climbing onto his lap.

Was the Master's magnetic joyousness a trait since birth, or was it the result of some unreported mystical experience before his public ministry began? I ask this question based on the dramatic changes in the lives of those who have had intense mystical experiences. In his book *The God We Never Knew,* scripture scholar Marcus Borg speaks of those who were suddenly engulfed by the awe-inspiring Divine Mystery in the midst of daily life. Borg tells the story of French philosopher Blaise Pascal: One night before midnight in 1654, Pascal had just such an experience in his own home that lasted a couple of hours. It was so profound that Pascal wrote it down on a piece of paper in telegraphic style:

> God of Abraham, God of Isaac, God of Jacob.
> Not of philosophers and the learned. Certitude, certitude.
> Emotion, Joy. . . . Joy! Joy! Joy! Tears of Joy. . . .
> My God . . . let me not be separated from thee for ever.

Three powerful, life-altering emotions flowed from what Pascal had experienced:

1) a happiness that was so wondrous as to bring tears,
2) an overpowering certitude of God's existence, and
3) a passionate desire never to be separated from its source.

For the rest of his life, Pascal carried that piece of paper on which he had written those words. At his death it was found in his pocket!

Borg also tells of an illiterate English evangelist from the nineteenth century named Billy Bray. Being no eminent philosopher, Bray described his personal experience of ecstatic joy:

> In an instant the Lord made me so happy
> that I cannot express what I felt. I shouted for joy. . . .
> Everything looked new to me, the people,
> the fields, the cattle, the trees. I was like a man
> in a new world. . . .

Borg relates yet another account of a mystical experience by a British clergyman named Leslie Weatherhead, who lived in the early half of the last century. Leslie was departing from London by train, riding in a third-class compartment, when the small compartment was suddenly filled with light and he felt caught up in some loving, triumphant, luminous purpose. Weatherhead reports being filled with ecstasy.

> All men were shining and glorious beings
> who in the end would enter incredible joy . . . an
> indescribable joy possessed me.

He judges that this luminous experience lasted only a few seconds but that it remained vividly present to him for more than fifty years. One curious thing about it, he said, was the sense of overwhelming love he felt:

This lingering feeling . . . I loved everyone
in that compartment. It sounds silly now,
but at the moment, I think I would have died
for any one of the people in that compartment.

Could the source of the Master's ability to radiate
joyfulness be some similar but unrecorded mystical
experience? Did his mystical experience fill him with
such ecstatic joy and light that he also felt impelled to
give his life for all whom he looked upon? As Pascal carried the brief written account of his mystical encounter
for the rest of his life, perhaps the Master carried a glorious memory of his ecstatic experience. Such a parallel
mystical episode could explain what motivated the very
human Jesus to become so divinely compassionate, loving, and self-giving.

The majority of us have not had such rapturous visitations, so what can motivate us to live joyfully? Life-changing ecstasies are gifts from God, not rewards given
for virtuous living. Neither are they achieved by deep
meditation. While you and I have not been so gifted, we
can learn from those special few who have had mystical
encounters that the Divine Mystery is usually experienced as passionate, euphoric happiness. If this, then, is
the predominant human experience of the inexpressible Mystery of God, can we not strive to live joyfully
as much as possible? Is this not our way of living in
God? While the imperative to "rejoice always" seems
beyond our human nature, perhaps it could be within
our reach if it were restated as, "Rejoice—be cheerful as
often as possible!"

Intimacy with God cannot be manufactured with mind-altering drugs, force of will, or long periods of extended meditation. Ironically, fidelity to living a happy and joyous life, regardless of the circumstances, may be the source of experiencing God! While what you experience may not be as unearthly as the reports of rapture by visionaries, it will be a taste of divine happiness. The vocational invitation is to become blind visionaries and find delight in the common things of daily life: in a sip of wine, a meal of friendship shared, the sight of a golden autumn oak, the silent splendor of a full moon rising, or the wondrous birth of a child. These all are mystical experiences. Each of these all too seemingly human joys, which are deeply relished and savored, also encourage us to strive to live happily by living in God. Millennia of sacred history confirm that God's desire is that the majority of us experience the mystical in the delights of taste, sight, sound, and touch of the ordinary. Blessed, then, are those who are not blind, deaf, or insensitive to the ordinary!

[1] John 1:35–42
[2] John 15:11
[3] John 16:22
[4] Luke 24:32

gargoyle gaiety

Side by side high up on the great French cathedrals are found conflicting stone images of angels and gargoyles. To place carved images of angels and saints on a cathedral is logical, but gargoyles? These grotesque, half-human, half-animal monsters seem totally inappropriate on God's House, especially those awesomely beautiful medieval cathedrals that were designed to be stone and glass visions of heaven come down to earth.

The name *gargoyle* comes from the gargling sound of rainwater pouring out of the open, often laughing mouths of these bizarre stone creatures that were actually gutter spouts intended to cast rainwater away from the building. Since there was no architectural reason to disguise gutter spouts, it must have been a bit of medieval holy comedy to put ugly monsters alongside the awe-inspiring angels and saints. English author

Malcolm Muggeridge believes their purpose was to express this delightful contradiction.

> Mystical ecstasy and laughter are the two great delights of living, and saints and clowns their purveyors, the only two categories of human beings who can be relied on to tell the truth. . . .

When Muggeridge appeared on American public television, he said that what we propose as being dignified and spiritually noble is actually ludicrous. He told the interviewer that everything under heaven was laughable: the Sistine Chapel, Mother Teresa of Calcutta, the great Chartres Cathedral, and Bach's Mass in B Minor. Especially ludicrous was the comedy of life that stripteases, revealing the naked outrageous gap between what humans aspire to and what they actually achieve. Naturally the interviewer and many of the viewers were scandalized by his remarks.

Here's a suggestion coined from Muggeridge's observation that everything under heaven is laughable: don't take too seriously your stumbling attempts at spiritual perfection, especially trying to live joyfully in all situations, since always is forever and a day! If you're yearning to be a saint, you must learn to play the clown. The next time you respond to some personal misfortune with anger or sadness instead of childlike glee, laugh aloud at yourself or at least break into a big smile. Self-humor, where you make yourself the subject of the joke, doesn't come easily or even naturally. Our childhood fear of being teased or ridiculed has tattooed us with a lifelong addiction to being respected and taken seriously by others. This subterranean addiction surfaces whenever you commit some blunder in front of others and their laughter at your mistake stings like burning acid. To address this addiction, strive to correct it by making fun of yourself when alone and with others.

Regardless of failures at poking fun at yourself, continue to at least chuckle at your spiritual clumsiness when you're impatient or uncharitable with others. Wholesome self-humor—being a holy work—requires the grace of the mirthful Spirit. If you pray seriously to this muse-spirit of life's divine comedy, you'll be given the grace to be silly. Yes, silly!

Now, please allow me an old man's prerogative of repeating himself and inserting here what I've written in a previous book about being silly. In Anglo-Saxon times, a "silly" person was one who was "blessed and innocent," and so holy. Saints were silly, as were peacemakers, the poor in spirit, and those hungry for justice. Since these holy ones of God were joyful people, the word *silly* began to mean "happy and unworldly." Unfortunately time was unkind to the word *silly*, and after many years it began to mean "foolish and ridiculous." This change from blessed to foolish was logical since the values of society also had changed, and never returning injury for injury and loving your enemies wasn't being blessed, it was just plain stupid and foolish. So then, those who were happy regardless of the occasion, especially when they suffered misfortune, just looked silly, simple-minded, and certainly not blessed. This is as true today as it was centuries ago. So pray to the Silly Spirit to become silly in the old-fashioned way, and never fear appearing foolishly blessed.

For example, you've set your heart on having an enjoyable picnic, spread a tablecloth out on the grass, and placed on it fried chicken and potato salad, and then suddenly the overcast sky splits wide open! As the rain in the days of old Noah pours down in torrents, tilt your head back and become a giggling gargoyle, letting the rainwater gush out of your mouth. And when the lightning flashes, followed by a deafening clap of thunder, listen carefully and you'll hear, "Blessed are you, my joyful silly beloved!"

the global echo,
"rejoice always"

Being joyful as a source of holiness isn't exclusive to Christian spirituality, since it is also the advice of spiritual guides in the Islamic, Jewish, Buddhist, Zen, Taoist, and Native American traditions. Any spiritual teaching that is global—that is catholic with a small "c"—confirms that it is a universal desire of God. The Spirit isn't the exclusive muse of any one religion and has never been partial in lavishly pouring out her gifts of inspiration.

Millennia ago the Greek playwright Euripides (480–406 BC) had a character in one of his plays say, "You were a stranger to sorrow: therefore Fate has cursed you." What a memorable line to recall the next time you feel the shroud of sorrow descend upon you. Not to know tearful sorrow is no blessing, as the

Greeks knew so well. Nor is it contrary to living in joy. Sorrow and joy are not incompatible, since there can be happiness in times of great sorrow and sorrow in joyful times. A spouse sorrowful at the death of a beloved companion can also rejoice that death has released his lover from the anguish of some long-suffered illness. Likewise, the victorious and humble athlete, while rejoicing at winning the gold, can lament that her worthy opponent didn't win. Joy and sorrow, like pain and pleasure, are interlinked in the human drama of life.

The question in that quote of Euripides is, "Who in this mortal life could ever be a stranger to sorrow?" Storytellers have created tales in which kings try to shelter their children from the sight of all human misery. These rulers carefully keep their children secluded behind palace walls, never to encounter the crippled and aged, the starving and sick, and the greatest of human sorrow—death. In one such legend, a young prince in India is carefully protected from all these sorrows, but escapes the protective enclosure in which he has been raised. Once out in the world, he discovers firsthand every conceivable horror and human sorrow. The young prince is so moved by what he sees that he becomes an ascetic and lives in solitude in the forest for years. By endless prayer and meditation he seeks the answer to the sorrowful miseries of existence. After seven years of meditating under a bo tree, he is enlightened to the deep mysteries of life. Awakened, he begins teaching a religious path, and so moved by its beauty are his listeners that they ask him if he is a god. He answers,

"No, I am awake, I am a *Buddha*, an Awakened One."

In India, five hundred years before Jesus, the teachings of the Buddha contained the very same admonition that we have from Paul: "live in joy."

Live in joy,
in love,
even among those who hate.

Live in joy,
in health,
even among the afflicted.

Live in joy,
in peace,
even among the troubled.

Health, contentment, and trust
are your greatest possessions,
and freedom your greatest joy.

Look within.
Be still.
Free from fear and attachment,
know the sweet joy of the way.

Buddha ranks freedom as the greatest of joys. Yet freedom is perhaps the most overlooked and neglected of gifts. Those who have spent years in prison, however, know the great joy of being free to do the ordinary things of daily life that the rest of us take for granted. Those who are now restricted to living in a nursing home, no longer able to drive an automobile or go wherever they wish when they wish, are also keenly aware of the loss of that greatest joy—freedom.

Buddha's challenge is to live in joy regardless of the circumstances, even when you find yourself among those who hate and are troubled. To remain steadfastly living in joy while those with whom you work are angry, negative, hostile, and argumentative is a test of the depth of your gladness. Those whose joy is only skin-deep require sunny days, friendly coworkers, pleasant situations, and good health to live in joy. If you wear only a happy face, then you can be assured that mean-ness, rudeness, and combative people will give you a radical face-lift, revealing your true face. Since achieve-ment of authentic happiness requires frequently return-ing to its source that resides within you, Buddha taught, "Look within. Be still." That return to the source can mean fifteen minutes of silent reflection or only fifteen seconds. The more frequently you return to the source, the easier it will be to do so in a few fleeting moments in order to be renewed by that life-nourishing contact.

Continue deepening your joy by following Buddha's wise advice to be "free from fear and attachment." When we are attached, overly emotionally connected, to our possessions or our ideas and opinions, we place our happiness in jeopardy. Regardless of whether it is your favorite chair, a brilliant idea, or some strong opin-ion, never cling to any of them. Hold them as loosely as you would sand in your hand so that if circumstances require, you can let them easily flow away. Buddha also instructs us to be free of fear, that crippling emotion connected with the threat of the loss of life, property,

reputation, and other intangible but precious possessions. The words of the Buddha about living in joy,
coming as they do from another religious tradition,
confirm our Christian challenge that to live in joy is
indeed the will of God for all peoples. A great cause for
rejoicing is that when it comes to sharing divine wisdom, the Spirit of God doesn't discriminate between
those of various religions or denominations, or even
between believers and nonbelievers.

The Buddha's teaching to "live in joy, in peace, even
among the troubled" is the litmus test of authentic joyful living. It is not difficult to be cheerful when you are
in the company of happy people who find life entertaining. But when you live with those who seem obsessively
dissatisfied, the test of happiness and contentment is
twofold. First, how do you remain joyful in their
midst? Second, what is the best way to express your
own cheerfulness?

If you encounter a neighbor or an acquaintance
notorious for being addicted to finding fault, instead of
politely trying to escape the person's company, rejoice
that you have been gifted with an experiment to test the
depth of your joy. This experiment becomes more difficult when the person is someone with whom you work
each day or with whom you live! A play on the Galilean
Master's words "If you love those who love you, what
credit is that to you?"[1] could be, "If you are joyful only
around those who are happy, what merit is there in
that?"

First, respond to the complaints, woeful predic-
tions, or apprehensions of failure by being silently

grateful for your personal practice of striving to live joyously. After taking a deep breath of silent thanksgiving, begin the second test: responding to the negativity. For chronic complainers, don't even attempt to cheer them up or try to help them see the other side of their ominously dark outlook. Chronic nitpickers suffer relentless faultfinding that may have begun in their childhood and now after many years has matured into an entrenched addiction. As useless as offering a glass of lemonade instead of a shot of whiskey to an alcoholic is trying to advise a gloomy person to look on the bright side of life.

Allow me to tell a story about chronic complainers. There is a woman, an atheist, who always grumbles about religion being a waste of time and a refuge for the weak-minded and timid. She enjoys ridiculing pious religious practices and beliefs with her left-wing friends. One day this woman takes her favorite little grandson to the beach. She puts a new swimsuit and a little hat on him, gives him a toy pail and shovel, and tells him to have fun. And as he does, she soon falls asleep in her beach chair.

Suddenly, a great wave sweeps upon the beach and drags the little boy out into the ocean, screaming. His loud cries awaken his grandmother, who goes crazy with panic and starts yelling, "Save my child! Save my child!" Looking around, she realizes no one is there; everyone else has gone home, and she is alone on the beach with her grandson being dragged farther and farther out into the ocean. She suddenly realizes, atheist or not, that she doesn't have much choice. Tilting her head back and throwing her arms heavenward she shouts, "Creator of the universe, I promise you if you save my grandson, I'll return to worshiping you each week. Forget what I've said about religion, I believe, I believe! Please save the child!"

At that moment a giant wave rises up in the ocean and picks up the child and carries him back crashing ashore on the beach. She runs down to him and sees that he's breathing and rejoices. But then suddenly she begins frowning. She looks up and points a finger skyward and shouts, "He had a hat!"

More than humorous, stories such as this one contain a great insight about how to respond to the pessimism of complainers as one would a precious gift. The story ends with her trivial challenging complaint to God about her grandson's hat. To her ranting, the heavens remained silent. So you likewise can respond with silent peace whenever you are confronted with complainers. In the company of those who bemoan and nitpick, live in peace—don't immigrate to their sad world of dissatisfaction. As kids we used to call older folks who always complained "crabby" and avoided them as best we could. But with age comes wisdom, or at least it should! Wisdom leads us to being compassionate toward those who are constant gripers and brings us the understanding that they are emotionally disabled. They perhaps have been crippled early in childhood by growing up in unhappy, gloomy homes. Over the years this sad childhood affliction has become habitual, and so an indelible part of their personality of self-pity.

Finding peace by living joyfully doesn't need to be expressed in words, and also need not create in us a need to convert others to happiness. It is only natural to wish that good friends or family members could experience the rich rewards of a joyful life. Unfortunately we cannot force them into that unique state of happiness that is not crippled by the daily difficulties of life. However, you can be a living invitation to immigrate to that Land of the Blessed! Your cheerfulness in the face of difficulties can be a non-threatening, non-preachy living invitation to share in the joyous life of God. Your living invitation doesn't require or even expect a response since it is really just a prayer of hope for the other's happiness.

Those whose lives are such invitations to the wedding feast of the bliss of heaven (the only kind of joy that is rust- and bulletproof) must not only be patient, they must be realistic. After the age of forty, and often even much younger than that, truly significant changes rarely occur in someone's personality. People at that age can experience religious conversions, but their basic personalities remain the same. Even so, do not abandon your hopeful desire that someone you love can have a conversion to living a positive, joyous life, since the Master taught that with God, all things were possible.

Meanwhile, by living cheerfully you can more easily and honestly truly love friends or family members. You love *them*, not as you would like *them* to be, but as *they* truly are—warts, gloom, negativity, and all. Living in joy is living in love, and in the hope that this person you so long to see joyful will someday be infallibly absorbed in Unconditional Joy. To live in such profound confidence illuminates your present joy like a sunrise with eternal splendor.

[1] Luke 6:32

kosher joyfulness

An encore of Paul's words to the Thessalonians is found in the "Be joyful always" of Jewish Hasidic mysticism. Ba'al Shem Tov, the founder of Jewish Hasidism, a mystical path to unity with God, taught that service to God requires the deepest joy. He taught, "Know that God's presence is with you," and encouraged his disciples to rejoice in that mysterious indwelling of their Creator who constantly beholds them with fascination and love. This joyfulness, he taught, can't be experienced in a divided self that separates the secular and sacred part of daily life, divides prayer from work, or disjoins the marketplace from the synagogue. Joy, like gratitude and prayer, requires a totality of life contained in that essential condition of "always" and "in all circumstances."

When this rabbi was challenged by his disciples to explain how it is possible to be deeply joyful when confronting your sins, he replied, "By denouncing excessive anxiety or brooding over one's sins." He taught that repetitive, sad grieving over our sins is a clever trick of the Evil One to keep us from God, the Blissful One. "Repent of evil," he would tell his astonished disciples. Yes, yes, repent—but then immediately return to being joyful and dancing before God.

The Spirit of God is like the wind that blows where and when it will. What is truly essential for holiness and unity with God isn't the sole property of any one religion or philosophy. The truth is that you can enrich your own spiritual path by incorporating devotions, prayers, and the wisdom of other religious traditions. This being true, let us pause to explore further Jewish Hasidic spirituality. Hasidism is a Jewish movement that originated in Eastern Europe in the eighteenth century. It is considered both spiritual and political, since it asserts the spirituality of the poorly educated classes against the elitism of the learned. Its prayer and worship is characterized by enthusiastic joy expressed in song, dancing, and prayer. The vitality of any religion resides in its ability to experience constant renewal. Hasidic Jews are keenly aware of the dangers of ritual prayer and liturgical rites that by their constant repetition easily become mechanical. The Hasidim teach that for communal prayer to be prayerful it has to be infused daily with great devotion and passionate love. Each time of prayer, even private prayer, is a call to enter into the fiery furnace of love.

Let the Spirit nudge you to learn from this Hasidic tradition and spice up your life and prayer with delight, and with a totality of heart and soul. Be creative, especially by altering traditional prayers to prevent them from becoming robotic. Hasidic masters teach the importance of beginning each new day like the first one in Eden. Each new day is a new creation, so when you get out of bed, let the first words on your lips be those of joyful gratitude. Since all the words one speaks each day have their roots in the first words spoken, let your first ones be those of joy to God!

For the Hasidim, being always joyful includes their prayer-conversations with God. We Christians are too prone to being formal and deferential in our prayer-conversations with God, especially in our communal worship. This Hasidic playfulness with the Almighty is found in the following story of the distinguished rabbi Levi Yitshak of Berdichev. Standing in the synagogue on the eve of most solemn Yom Kippur, he prayed, "O Holy One, in a few hours the Jews are coming to ask you for forgiveness for all their sins and many wrongdoings. But I want to give you, the All Holy One, a chance to be forgiven for all the terrible wrongs that you've done."

Rabbi Yitshak then proceeded to rattle off a long litany of divine visitations of evils: the deaths of innocent small children, crippling illnesses and plagues, vicious anti-Semitic attacks on Jewish homes and shops. He continued on and on until reaching the end of his long list of God's wrongdoings, when he concluded, "Are you not God, responsible for all that happens?" Rabbi Yitshak then paused and looked heavenward and said, "So God, let's make a deal: we'll let you off the hook—if you'll let us off."

The daring familiarity of this prayer of Rabbi Yitshak reveals his deeply personal, intimate friendship with God that allowed him to be playfully cheerful in prayer on the eve of one of Israel's most solemn high holy days. His intimacy with God challenges us to both pray and play with God, using words of familiarity and delight. If your personal prayers are modeled upon solemn liturgical patterns, then they will be as stiffly formal as if you were addressing some Roman emperor. So, boldly and blessedly energize them with a little kosher humor and profound joy.

thirty-two

leaking laughter
as you go

An old and good friend, Mary Kay Meyer, the director of the Catholic Worker House in Kansas City, Kansas, sent me a quote of an Islamic holy man she had read in *I Heard God Laughing*, Daniel Ladinsky's book of the sayings of Hafiz.

> Bring your cup near me,
> for I am a sweet old vagabond
> with an infinite leaking barrel
> of light and laughter and truth
> that the Beloved has tied to my back.

Age, arthritis, and the constant pull of gravity can cause the heads and shoulders of older people to begin bending forward. Perhaps this condition inspired these beautiful words by Hafiz, whose name means "one who knows the Koran by heart." Intriguing is his image of the large barrel tied to his back. Was the author of that mystical prayer stooped over by age or osteoporosis? If he was, then he is a holy example of embracing with good humor and playfulness that aged affliction of a humped back by seeing it as a barrel brimming with laughter and light given him by his Beloved Allah. If you have also begun to feel that inclination of aging to stoop a bit—with the weight of your head being slightly tilted downward by gravity and old age—imitate old Hafiz and begin to see yourself as also carrying on your back a leaking barrel of mirth and light. Regardless of your posture, if you zealously seek to be constantly happy, everywhere you go you also will carry a leaking barrel of light, laughter, and truth.

Several lines of Hafiz's prayer are particularly heart touching—"bring your cup near me"—for they express the desire of anyone living joyfully to share their happiness with others. "Bring your cup near . . ." implies "and come fill that cup of yourself with my good humor, laughter, and cheerfulness, since I have an infinite supply of them." No joyful person ever desires to hoard his or her happiness. This makes it totally unlike other forms of wealth. Delight in life is divinely paradoxical, since it creates an enthusiastic desire to give away to others as much of it as possible.

Visually charming is the image "an infinite leaking barrel" as a metaphor of his abundance of joy that is constantly and unconsciously leaking out laughter and light wherever he goes. The Sufis were the wandering, vagabond Muslim mystics, the barefoot Franciscan poor men of Islam. Wherever they roamed, they left a trail of mirth and luminosity by their joyfulness and passionate love of God. The Sufis understood that the most powerful influence of true spiritual masters was simply their presence! Not brilliant or poetic insights, memorable quotations, or moving sermons on passages of the holy book, but the joyfulness of their lives was their greatest influence upon others. Those who place importance on the shrewdness of their arguments or wise insights need to be reminded that 99 percent of spoken words have a life span of three to five seconds! The wind is a vast, silent-swaying cemetery of dead words! But what really stains the souls of those who come in contact with any holy person—be he a friend, parent, or pastor—is the light and joyfulness unconsciously leaking out of them!

Light and joyfulness are joined at the hip, since light-hearted people are optimistic, cheerful, and happy. When people such as these find themselves in dark situations, the inner light seeping out of them is as reassuring as the brilliance of a flashlight in a blackout. In all great spiritual traditions, the Divine Mystery, while known by countless holy names, is also universally known as Light. Lighthearted people then are Godhearted people, and only the Godhearted leak God. Since they don't generate their own light, their luminosity never dims regardless of how dark or dismal are the eclipses of daily events. Light- and laughter-leaking disciples of the Master are not spin doctors, those surgeons of sad situations so named for their deceptive skills of putting a positive spin on something bad. The

White House, large corporations, and the military have emergency rooms staffed 24/7 with highly skilled spin surgeons.

Surprisingly, this form of situation plastic surgery isn't restricted to instututional propaganda. A majority of people, it seems, feel a compelling need to practice spin medicine. Whenever others share with them their own difficulties, these folk healers feel an urgent need to put a positive twist on the other person's problems. It seems that this usually subconscious need to try to help the troubled person by proposing something positive about their problems may arise from feeling pity or misguided compassion. There is that very human need to do "something" to help those with problems. This need seems to be answered by attempting to help them find a bright side to their dark problems. This doesn't really help, of course, since it is misguided compassion. While the desire to be compassionate is valid, the comfort that is offered is imprudently untimely.

What really does give comfort to those who are burdened is simply a full-hearted listening to their laments over their sad situation. A wise listener knows that when someone is burdened by misfortune, his or her greatest need is simply to talk about it and to be heard. Non-advice-giving listening heals by being supportive and sympathetic. Silent spin doctors heal the best! These healers spin—they rotate their attention away from themselves so as to fully focus on the other person's needs. They are also leaking doctors who know from experience that by their fully attentive listening presence, in person or on the telephone, the Light seeps out of them.

The third grace leaking out of Hafiz's barrel, after laughter and light, is truth, which at first seems oddly unconnected to the other two. Upon closer reflection, however, it is the perfect completion to that leaking holy trinity, since the truth is this: God is eternal laughter and light! Blessed then are those who—finding themselves bruised and battered from that often bumpy ride on the roller coaster of life—not only hear God laughing, but join in.

thirty-three

hey **old clod,** what now?

From the Taoist tradition of ancient China comes another echo of the Spirit's call to joyfulness in life, regardless of the circumstances. An old holy man named Master Hu, a follower of the way of Tao, lived long, long ago in ancient China. Old Hu loved God, and God loved Hu. So whatever God did was fine with Old Hu, and whatever Hu did was fine with God, since they were such good friends. Being good friends, Hu and God liked to kid around, and Hu would jokingly call his friend God "the Great Clod." That was fine with God, who would joke with Hu in return, like give him warts on his face, arthritis in his hands and feet, a canker sore in his mouth, and even gout in his feet. God was a great kidder, and that was fine with Old Hu, since they were such good friends.

As a result of God's numerous jokes, old Master Hu grew lumpy as a toad and crooked as a human pretzel.

"You Old Clod," Hu would shout at God, laughing, and that was fine with God. Just to show his old friend Hu that he was listening, God made Hu's right leg ten inches shorter than his left, and that made Old Hu walk around in little circles. Laughing loudly, Master Hu would say to the villagers, "Ha ha! See how the Great Clod listens to me! Look how ugly and silly I'm becoming," and looking up to the sky, "Hey, Old Clod, you make me laugh and laugh, but that's what friends are for."

This only caused the villagers to wag their heads at Master Hu, and their tongues too, saying, "Old Hu has gone crazy!" Hearing that, he winked at them, and looked up to the sky, shouting, "Hey Clod! Are you awake or not? What's next?" And zap, out popped a fresh wart. Seeing his newest affliction, the villagers walked away convinced that Old Hu was crazy, and maybe he was. Had God also sent craziness down on him, along with his warts, arthritis, and gout? If so, it didn't bother Old Hu; it was just fine with him since he loved God and God loved him.

So as the years jogged by one after another, Old Hu became the most twisted, arthritic, wart-covered, ugly, happy old man in all of China. Then, one day, casting a cataract-clouded eye heavenward, he whispered, "Hey Clod! What now?" And God reached down his hand and drew Old Hu right up unto Himself. And that was just fine with Hu. That's what a Friend is for.

Among the stories and parables of earth's religions, this Taoist parable has to be one of the finest illustrations of the imperative to be joyful regardless of the circumstances. Taoism was an early spiritual path of ancient China based on the teachings of Lao-tse, who lived in the sixth century BC. The *Tao*, or "The Way," emphasizes simplicity in spiritual practice and fosters living in harmony with nature by seeking a balance in life of the male and female principles of creation. This story of Master Hu is short, so consider reading it a second time, slowly and aloud, since it vibrates with great power. The tale of Hu expresses the unconditional source of how to be always joyful regardless. The litany of miseries visited upon old Hu resemble those God bestowed on mythical, poor Job in the Old, or First, Testament. Unlike poor Job, Master Hu could laugh and joke with God about his heaven-sent misfortunes. This rare ability was clearly the result of his deep, intimate friendship with God, whom Hu treated like a true friend.

When confronted with painful difficulties or a serious illness, such an intimate, trusting relationship with the Divine Mystery is the source of enduring happiness. Mirthfully dealing with your miseries isn't the same as stoically enduring them. To live in joy requires living in trust that your Divine Friend will creatively convert whatever is unpleasant in your life into something good. Trust is a deeply confident reliance upon another who has proven in past experiences to be truly trustworthy. This kind of trust is the fruit of love and intimate friendship. Master Hu and God were friends! Master Hu dealt with his endless misfortunes with gleeful humor because of his unshakable love and trusting assurance that God loved him as a dearest friend.

It would be understandable to disregard this Taoist tale as humorous but impractical in the real world, since it's only a story. No Master Hu ever existed! That's true! And likewise there was never a real Good Samaritan or Prodigal Son either. Those stories, like that of Master Hu, are teaching parables, life patterns to show us how to behave, and also how God behaves!

holy humorous **communion**

In the previous Taoist parable, Master Hu's response to his afflictions was prayerful laughter! Instead of somber acceptance of his fate or some prayerful groaning, "Thy will be done," he responded to God with laughing. Laughter is certainly not one of the traditional religious forms of dialogue with God. Yet laughter has the great power to cement relationships.

Dr. Robert Provine, a professor of neuroscience and psychology at the University of Maryland, calls laughter social glue. He says that the laughter you hear in various daily gatherings is more than a response to something humorous. Dr. Provine believes that human laughter is more closely related to the calls of wild animals that help them to bond together into groups. Each time you engage in laughter with others over a joke or

some humorous event, you are becoming more connected with them. If laughter then is instrumental in
connecting humans with one another, why could it not
also bind us more deeply in our human-divine relationship with God?

Laughter is both liberating and a simple mechanism
for living in the present moment, as the Zen scholar R.
H. Blyth says:

> Laughter is a state of being here and also everywhere,
> an infinite and timeless expansion of one's nevertheless
> inalienable being. When we laugh, we are free of all
> the oppression of our personality, or that of others, and
> even of God, who is indeed laughed away.

Blyth's insight about laughter's liberating power is
true, since it not only deflates our overblown false self-
image, but also our false Christian image of a solemn,
imperial God.

Moshe Waldoks, a Jewish author and scholar of
Eastern European Jewish history, echoes these Zen
insights about laughter:

> I've yet to hear of anyone doing a humor meditation,
> but humor and meditation accomplish the same
>   aims.
> Both help to let everything float away—they show
>   you that you are not the center of the universe.

If prayer is union with God and laughter naturally
bonds humans together, wouldn't laughter then be a
prayer of an exceptionally potent Holy Communion?

Couldn't laughter, because of its psychological power
to deepen interpersonal bonds, unite us more intimately with God than ritualistic communion, regardless of
our faith in what it is that we receive? This question
could be disturbing to orthodox believers, but it
shouldn't be, for it does not imply that a devout, faith-
filled reception of Holy Communion isn't a uniting act
with Christ. The question also doesn't mean replacing
frequent receptions of Holy Communion with frequent
laughing. The question is a parable. What it is proposing isn't one form of communion over another, but the
practice of both frequent Merry Communions and
Holy Communions.

Most people receive Holy Communion only once a
week or seasonally, but Merry Communion can easily be
generously sprinkled numerous times throughout each
day. Whenever you discover yourself acting pompous or
stumbling awkwardly physically or verbally—laugh
at yourself, and do so in humorous Holy Communion
with God. Merry Communion is a mystical encounter,
a physical contact with the Divine Spirit of happiness.
Blest are those who rejoice always, since they are in continuous Merry Communion.

Since prayer is a form of communion, consider
including some laughter in your personal daily prayers.
Imagine beginning your prayer with a brief chuckle, saying, "Well Old Friend, here I am again, begging at your
door." A chuckle is a meditative, quiet laughter often
hardly audible, but it contains the same bonding powers of a full belly laugh. To smile broadly each time you
make the Sign of the Cross can be your personal

witnessing to the truth of that Good Friday chant, "Behold the wood of the cross wherein joy came into the world." If indeed the cross of Jesus ushered joy into our woe-begotten world, then to trace the sign of that cross upon yourself while making an expression of joy would be a statement of faith in the happy harvest of the cross.

Some orthodox believers could deem connecting the cross of Christ with laughter or even a smile as scandalous, since there wasn't anything funny about his passion and death. Yet it is the Easter eggs, lilies, and water rituals of the Easter liturgy that dynamically symbolize a Christian belief that the death and resurrection of Jesus Christ inaugurated a new creation. A laughing Alleluia is divinely appropriate, for, as René Daumal said, "I know that in the beginning Chaos was ignited by an immense burst of laughter."

waraiko prayer

The Japanese have a centuries-old ritual called *Waraiko* they use to greet a new year and to celebrate birthdays. The ritual consists of giving three hearty belly laughs! The first robust laugh is of gratitude for the previous year just ended. The second hearty laugh is in gratitude for being given a new year of life to enjoy. The third is a really full-bodied belly laugh, since it is to blow the dust off your mind, heart, and soul. Dust? The dust of habit and routine that slowly accumulates like all dust, causing the soul to lose the luster of its youthful vitality.

Instead of restricting the *Waraiko* ritual only to New Year's Eves and birthdays, consider the possibilities of using this ritual of three hearty laughs as your morning prayer. At the beginning of a new day, your first prayer laugh would be in gratitude for all the gifts of yesterday and a good night's sleep. Your second laugh could be for the wondrous gift of a new day of life overflowing with opportunities to enjoy it fully. The third and most boisterous laugh would be to blow the dust off your soul so it and your heart can glisten like the rising sun. For some, just after arising may be too early an hour in the day for a good laugh, especially a high-quality belly laugh, so consider using its humorous cousin, a good chuckle with a broad smile.

Chuckling is also a sign of gladness and creates the breeze of delight that can blow the dust off your soul, causing it to gleam again like new. There is a valid connection between dusting and gladness, since the original meaning of *glad* was, "gleaming, shining, and bright!" Perhaps because cheerful people had a special luminous shimmer to their faces, *glad* came to mean "happy, joyful, and pleasant." Since laughing for no apparent good reason is usually considered a sign of being giddy or a scatterbrain, wisely do as the Master taught. When you pray, go in your room, close the door, and pray in secret. While sage advice for any prayer, it's especially true for *Waraiko* prayer. If you faithfully observe this prayer rule of praying in secret and someone actually does observe you at your Waraiko morning prayer, don't be concerned if they think you are giddy!

The goal of every religious seeker should be to be giddy since in Old English it once meant "possessed by a god or spirit." Being possessed by the Spirit wasn't such a desirable state, since those caught in the grip of God were considered to be insane, simple-minded, or religious fanatics. In time the word changed from connoting foolish to being incapable of serious thinking.

And you can be assured that if you strive to be constantly cheerful, even in the most dismal of situations, you will be judged as a shallow thinker or at best uninformed. After all, who can be always joyful if they live in the "real" world?

The Church, preoccupied with the need to be taken seriously by the world, is constantly cautious of appearing as foolish or silly, and so has wisely limited celebrating rejoicing to only two Sundays out of the year. One comes in the middle of Advent and in the Old Latin is called *Gaudete*, "Rejoice" Sunday. The second one comes in the middle of Lent and was called *Laetare* Sunday, also Latin for "rejoice." To live in joy, which Paul said was the will of God for us, seems to require a change in the Church's liturgical calendar. To remind the faithful of their duty to remain joyful while confronting all of the terrible sufferings plaguing the human family—wars, violence, famine, and global poverty—the Church should have at least one *Gaudete-Laetare* Sunday a month! Such monthly Joy Sundays would reinforce that God's will be done on earth as it is in heaven!

the joys of
visiting the **mall**

Dining comes in second place as Americans' favorite activity right after the pleasures of shopping. The folk prescription when you find yourself down in the dumps and feeling blue is "go buy something." Visiting the mall, the modern version of the marketplace, is for many as therapeutic as visiting their doctor. Some studies report that the favorite activity of overworked Americans on vacation isn't doing nothing—but shopping!

Four centuries before the birth of Jesus, Greek philosopher Socrates also found enjoyment in going to the busy marketplace of Athens. Strolling through the many stalls of vendors and viewing the vast array of things they offered for sale, Socrates would rejoice, saying, "Ah, how many things I have no need of!" To stroll with your spouse or a friend through a crowded mall or along the sidewalk past shops selling a vast array of beautiful things can be a prayerful, enjoyable experience. If you have a heart as contented as that of Socrates, you can smile and joyfully say, "Ah, how many things I have absolutely no need of. Oh, I'm so fortunate!"

I recently accompanied a friend to the drugstore, and as he waited in a long line at the checkout counter, I wandered around the store. Each aisle held head-high shelves filled with little boxes, bottles, and tubes of all kinds of remedies, painkillers, and assorted over-the-counter medicines. Simply reading the labels was a revelation for me into the countless afflictions and ailments confronting humanity: hair loss, constipation, incontinence, aches and pains in every part of the body. At that moment I had a drugstore epiphany! I was graced to recall the words of Socrates about visiting the marketplace. Standing in the midst of all those medicinal remedies for distressing, painful afflictions, I grinned, "I rejoice and give you thanks God, since how many, if not almost all, of these things I have no need of!"

The third in the famous trinity of holy imperatives from Paul is, "Give thanks always and in all circumstances." Close to first place in your daily litany of thanksgiving should be giving thanks for your "good" health; that is as good as possible since each age in life from adolescence to old age has its own bodily troubles. If you have ever desired to go on a pilgrimage and knew you couldn't afford the cost of flying to Rome or the

Holy Land, here's a proposal for a prayerful pilgrimage that's free! Make a pilgrimage to your neighborhood pharmacy or drugstore and prayerfully stroll the aisles, rejoicing in gratitude for all the many medicines you don't need! I assure you that you will return home holier and happier.

thirty-seven

being **joyful**— everywhere!

Old spiritual books usually concluded with reflections on the Last Things: death, heaven, and hell. Out of fear of being seduced into sin, Christians have rigidly steeled themselves against enjoying too much of the natural pleasures of good food and drink, and the God-given exotic pleasures of sexuality. For many, the Christian life has therefore been as perilous as walking a high wire across the gaping chasm of the Grand Canyon. The slightest slip might plunge one into the bottomless, fiery abyss of hell. Paul's use of "always" in his call to be joyful implies all circumstances. This raises the question, "Does that really mean all places?"

Johnny Carson once said that he found Carl Reiner's book *My Anecdotal Life: A Memoir,* "funny as

hell!" While hell conjures up all kinds of images of tor-
turous flames, unrelenting pain, and suffering, being a
funny place is never one of them. Johnny Carson's
descriptive use of "hell" to express his ultimate degree
of enjoyment in Reiner's book is not uncommon. *Hell*
is frequently used in contemporary speech to express
an extreme degree of anything: it rained like hell; it was
hot as hell, noisy as hell, or crowded as hell.
Surprisingly, our contemporary speech doesn't use
heaven as the ultimate degree of anything: funny as
heaven, cheerful or pleasant as heaven, or even crowded
as heaven! Is this because more people unconsciously
believe in the existence of hell than in that of heaven?
While we've all experienced hell here on earth, have we
done the same with heaven or what we think heaven
will be like? While we hope for a heaven of bliss and
peace, do we secretly fear that the next life will only be
a continuation of this life of hell on earth? Regardless
of your answer to that hypothetical question, returning
to Johnny Carson's description of Reiner's book, why
can't hell be fun?

On August 13, 2003, New York City experienced a
massive citywide electrical outage that trapped people
for hours in the hot, suffocating darkness of subways
and elevators. To be trapped in pitch-black darkness in
a crowded elevator car perilously dangling from the
cables can be terrifying beyond description. In one such
case that day in New York, a television news station
reported the rescue of those trapped in a stalled elevator car. They told how firefighters broke through the
escape hatch on the roof of one dangling elevator car

and that the first person rescued was a small five-year-old boy. After the firefighters had brought the small boy up to street level, a news reporter asked him what it was like being trapped in the elevator? With a big smile, he said, "It was fun!"

Why didn't this child experience being trapped in that dark elevator as frightening? How did he not experience it as hell instead of fun? A mature adult could answer that by saying, "Well, the boy was only five years old! At that age he couldn't possibly grasp the serious implications of the dangers involved." While that could be a correct answer, wouldn't a small child of five actually find it even more threatening than adults would? Wouldn't a small child naturally sense the terrible fright and anxieties of his fellow adult passengers trapped in that hellish total darkness? People respond differently to disasters, whether it's being trapped in an elevator or riding out a hurricane. Some are able to remain stoically calm, suppressing their natural fears, while others burst into weeping, fearing their death. There are others who take command of the situation, assuming the role of saviors, and seek some way of escape from the disaster in order to quiet their own fears. Then there are those who, for some unexplained reason, do not panic, but rather are able to experience a disaster as high adventure. These rare few have an unquenchable thirst and hunger for adventure. Perhaps they were the ones who as teenagers ran away to join the circus, or at least wanted to do so. These are the men and women who are intoxicated by high-octane, death-defying challenges: climbing the peaks of the

Himalayas or going on expeditions into the deepest jungles of the Amazon. At what age does this hunger for high adventure begin? At five years old? Or perhaps could it be a gift of birth? Since fear, being prehistoric, is such an abiding emotion in life, how is it possible to live both in the joy of adventure and in fearful dread?

The act of being birthed is painful for both child and mother. And while it can be frightening for the mother, it surely must be so for the infant coming forth from the comfortable security of the womb into a strange, unknown world. While we as adults have no conscious memory of the pains of our birth, that doesn't mean they don't still linger subconsciously within us. Along with this frightening birthing experience, in our subterranean inner depths could also be our communal prehistoric memory of surviving in an extremely hostile, dangerous world, where the slight snap of a twig could signal the approach of one's death. Is it possible that these two subconscious memories, along with all the numerous actual dangers of life itself, could explain our human disposition to be fearful? So universal and prevailing is this subterranean human fear that the Master repeatedly said, "Do not be afraid!"

Christians lay claim to the gift of two births, although most cannot remember either one. Along with your natural birth, the baptismal birthing event incorporates one into Christ. Do you inherit from him his courageous spirit in this second birth, or is that waterbirth only a spiritual, religious ritual conferring none of his personal qualities? Even if nothing is inherited by this baptismal birth, it is clear from the Master's words that he desired his disciples to imitate him. If you already possess the latent potential to act like him, then the challenge is to awaken those slumbering baptismal characteristics of Christ. As in life, where some natural talents appear early while others slumber until later in adulthood, so the same can be true of the baptismal traits of Christ: his prayerfulness, compassion, humility, and fearlessness. For some these traits appear in early adulthood, for others in their late thirties, midlife, or even later. At whatever age, once they have been stirred awake, diligence and discipline are required to mature them.

There is a second option that is the way of discipleship, which the Master expressed when he said, "Learn from me; [I am the lesson] for I am gentle and humble in heart."[1] True disciples strive to imitate their spiritual Master by enfleshing his teachings in themselves. Lacking textbooks, the disciples of Jesus learned their lessons by heart. The ancient Greeks and Hebrews believed that the heart was the seat of intelligence and emotions. This timeless belief is the source of our word *record* that originally meant "to memorize." In Latin *re,* "again," and *cor,* "heart," the lesson was recorded or learned by passing it again and again through the heart. Consider recording, or learning by heart, some of the Master's lessons like "do not be afraid [of anything][2] . . . I am with you always.[3] . . . Do not fear. Only believe. . . ."[4]

Develop the habit of repeating them like a chant whenever others attempt to make you live in fear for political or other reasons. Let one or the other echo again and again in your heart whenever you are confronted by something that is frightening. These memorized sayings of Jesus have power: they can conjure up his courageous spirit, which will inspire you to imitate him and banish your fears. They will remind you that you are one with God and so have nothing to fear. Then whenever you are forced to confront a disaster, you can respond like that five-year-old boy trapped in the elevator. This intimate oneness with God and the Teacher that gifts you the adventuresome Spirit also makes it possible to rejoice, even in hell!

[1] Matthew 11:29
[2] Matthew 10:31, Luke 2:10, and Luke 12:32
[3] Matthew 28:20
[4] Luke 8:50

escape or engage
in evolution

This reflection is intended to set you free from that almost impossible assignment of always living in joy, of being happy regardless of the circumstances. So rejoice—there's a fire escape from that impracticable imperative of Thessalonians, and it's evolution!

The spiritual maturing of the human family is evolutionary, as is all of creation, and as is each individual's personal spiritual growth. This gradual development of your inner life is evident by a brief examination of your life history. How you imagine and pray to God now is far different from how you did at age seven, or even sixteen, and likewise your moral values and ethical judgments have also matured. This same gradual growth process has also been the case with religion.

Death by stoning was once the accepted religious punishment for adultery, while loaning money at interest was condemned as a grave offense against God. From the bloody butchering of animals in sacrifice, the worship of God evolved to the table meal of the Lord's Supper, or a service of scripture reading, prayer, and praise. While religion over the millennia evolved slowly, a few unique individuals were able to rapidly advance spiritually far beyond the development of their contemporaries. In all the great religious traditions, a few persons have made large strides forward in their spiritual evolution into Godhood: saints, mystics, and spiritual masters. Unlike these few enlightened ones, the vast majority of us have struggled to simply maintain the minimum requirements of the moral code. It seems that each religion accepted and accepts this minimum observance of the moral laws, along with a weekly worship requirement, as being sufficient for their members. While religion elevates those few who have evolved to the status of saviors and saints, it does not seriously challenge the majority to imitate them. A similar failure to evolve in the natural world would have resulted in extinction, but not in religion! Ninety-nine percent of religious adherents settle for simply being good, instead of zealously striving to become saints. Good isn't good enough! It is inadequate when you are called to love God with all your heart and soul, and to apply that same degree of intensity to your spiritual evolution.

Unlike the rest of creation, humans not only have the ability to evolve upward into higher states of

Godhood, but they also have the grace to do so! This grace, a share in God's life, is given to everyone. The cosmos and we are designed to be constantly evolving, advancing upward in our maturity as daughters and sons of the Creator. Along with this power to continue developing, we have been given a pattern for our growth in Jesus of Galilee. We are a gifted yet also handicapped people. First, we are gifted with the grace-energy to progress toward greater and greater spiritual maturity. Second, we're given the contradictory gift of freedom! This divine gift is contra-evolutionary, for it allows us to refuse to grow up and evolve and to so remain stunted humans.

An example of our retarded evolutionary growth is our love of war, our pride in making wars and winning them, and our glorifying of warriors, depicting them as heroes in films and literature. If we truly understood that we as humans are by divine design also an integral part of evolution, then would not the heroes of our society be those who had outgrown their primitive urges for aggression, violence, and destruction? The Master unambiguously presented our evolutionary pattern in his teaching, saying we are to love our enemies, never return injury for injury, and instead do good to those who injure or offend us! Clearly, here is the Designer's blueprint for how we are to outgrow the prehistoric behavior of interpersonal violence, acts of clan or tribal revenge, and war between nations, as well as the barbaric practice of capital punishment.

A similar call to evolution confronts us with another divine design for growth: "Rejoice always, for this is the will of God for you." The cosmic call of the Creator to all creation is found in this saying of the Jewish Talmud: "Every blade of grass has its angel that bends over it and whispers, 'grow, grow.'" Not only does every blade of grass hear that divine whisper of the Spirit, but each of us also hears it each time we face the choice between acting only humanly and acting like God. While humanity seems to have achieved its maximum physical evolution, we have only begun to advance spiritually. To live a joyful life, being happy regardless of how difficult are the circumstances, is another of the destinations in our unfolding growth.

This is an achievable goal. It can be accomplished when you have awakened to who you really are. It is possible to live joyfully instead of as an exile in that mournful valley of tears, condemned to carry the heavy burden of existence, which is how too many view life. To become a saint is also possible, since the seed of that destination is in your heart. The evolutionary work of fulfilling your potential to achieve Godliness is not what has been proposed by those of former ages— transcending the world. Rather, it is waking up to who and where you are. More saturated than a sponge soaking with water, you have been absorbed by the Divine Mystery, by absolute bliss, joy, and happiness. You live, breathe, and work in a creation and world that is God-immersed. To awaken to these two awesome truths is to discover that you live, breathe, and work in joy. Dogmas have little if any effect on the quality of our daily lives, and so if this awareness of your oneness with and in

God is simply an intellectual thought, then you will not live a joyful life, except in your head!

While God-energy, or grace, is given to each person to spur him or her on their evolutionary path, it must be accompanied with an ardent desire to actually advance forward. While in the physical body growth is spontaneous, the inner development required to live a joyful life requires passionate desire and determined commitment to growth if you are to advance beyond your present stage. The reason for this is that growing upward toward God requires prevailing against a prehistoric condition of negative, fearful living.

thirty-nine

live **fearfully**—or die!

This next-to-the-last reflection continues the previous one with our evolutionary growth pitted against our prehistoric conditioning. Use your imagination to return to those dangerous, primal cave-dwelling times when human survival depended upon perpetual vigilance, upon being negatively suspicious about every single aspect of daily life. A snap of a twig behind you in the forest was a legitimate cause of fear, since it could mean an approaching wild beast or an enemy from another clan coming to attack you. Tens of thousands of years ago primitive humans were conditioned by their dangerous environment to live constantly anxious and fearful, and to be suspicious of everything and everyone. This made it possible for them to respond instantly to threats and dangers. Scientists today know that our strongest and fastest human responses are to dangers, threats, and objectionable

situations. These are more difficult for us to block than
are our responses to pleasurable situations. Our prehistoric ancestors, lacking control over their lives, were
constantly apprehensive of potentially deadly dangers.
If you had lived in those primitive days and sought to
live a joyful life by having a positive attitude toward
everything and everyone, your life span would have
been very short!

It seems that humans are permanently conditioned,
hard-wired so to speak, to focus on the negative. This
inherited trait is a result of the human family's emotional history of living for millennia in ruthless and
dangerous environments. So the next time you
encounter gloomy, fearful people with a pessimistic
outlook on life, realize that they are only being
human—prehistorically human. When you find it difficult to associate with family members or coworkers
because they are always so negative, try to be compassionate, since they are only responding to their human
preconditioning. The gospel challenge of the New
Testament, "Be always joyful," is radically evolutionary,
since it requires viewing the conditions of life and other
people with a positive outlook. That is radically different from being preconditioned to behave. Yet are not
the Master's teachings all evolutionary, commands to
advance upward beyond our prehistoric conditioning
of living in anxiety and fear?

We do not live in caves! To always live in joy in the
late 1800s would have required a miracle greater than the
changing of water into wine at the wedding feast of
Cana. In America at that time, the majority of laborers

worked a sixty-hour, six-day workweek. Transit laborers in Chicago worked eighty-four-hour weeks, and bakers worked one-hundred-twenty-hour weeks! The vast majority of their families endured harsh, cramped, and deprived living conditions. Preceding centuries saw unimaginably brutal working and living conditions for the common people throughout much of the world. In many places, these continue even today. Modern television and computer technology allow us to witness the lives of people in the developing world who are burdened by the harshest poverty, including starvation, epidemic disease, and intertribal brutality. We in developed countries, regardless of how poor we may be compared with our nearest neighbors, are wealthy, fortunate people indeed.

The past two centuries have witnessed swift and amazing advancements in technology and science that radically changed daily life for those living in first world countries. Americans of today would have been greatly envied by people in previous centuries, especially those of the first century after Jesus, when Paul's letters to the Thessalonians were written. For them, as for those today in poverty-ridden nations across the globe, it would be hard to see why it would be difficult for us to be happy and always joyful with all our creature comforts. No primal wild beasts lie in wait outside dwellings to devour us. We do not have go out to hunt for our food, gather firewood, or be forced to survive on berries. Many of us in the first world enjoy carefree, comfortable lives, automatically heated and cooled homes, only a five-day workweek, with ample leisure time and vacations, easily accessible and excessive food, clean drinking water, and readily available medical care. Those of previous ages and those in today's poor nations would surely wonder, "When they live like kings and queens, what prevents them from living in joy?"

The answer is that prehistoric conditioning! Still present deep within us is our inherited cave dweller's attitudes of fearfulness and negativity toward life. The inability to enjoy—to live happily with—our comfortable and relatively carefree lives is because our spiritual growth hasn't evolved with our rapid and highly developed technology. We have also failed to observe the second command of the Thessalonian trinity, "Give thanks constantly—regardless of the circumstance." Those who are always giving thanks for something, if not for everything, drastically reduce that primitive negativity that causes the mind to focus on failings, fears, and apprehensions.

Happiness is the fruit of addiction. Being joyful is the result of habitually giving thanks for the simplest gifts of life: a warm bed or a good night's sleep, the warmth of sunlight on your skin, a roof over your head on a rainy night, or the face of a friend. On and on go the daily occasions for joy. Like all addictions, this obsession with being grateful needs to grow as you age until you become an impossible drunk of delightful gratitude. By continuously thinking grateful thoughts for the gifts of daily life (and the wise know that everything is a gift), the mind has the power to transform negative thoughts into positive ones of joy. One of the secrets of happiness then is being obsessively and continuously grateful.

This thanksgiving trait requires not an evolutionary but a cultural development, since it requires denying the illegitimate desires induced by the media advertisers of our consumer society. Those gratefully satisfied with what they already possess tend to reject as the source of happiness anything that can be purchased. They know instead that happiness is the fruit of good personal relationships, love, and life's simple pleasures. Another byproduct of gratitude is that embracing gifts creates an instinctive desire to give them away, to be generous with your time and your self. Volunteered service to neighbor or stranger creates the condition of becoming absorbed in the other's life and needs, which then gifts one with the delightful state of self-forgetfulness. The infallible source of joy and happiness is healthy absent-mindedness of self that occurs whenever you are totally absorbed in an activity: service to others, creating art or music, cooking, being engrossed in poetry, praying, or dancing. So find as many ways as possible to become totally immersed in life, and you will find that you've become joy soaked. Because of that, you will also become holy.

Within each of us is an evolutionary seed of a potential saint. Our destiny and happiness require the cultivation of that seed with loving care. Already active is that creative process of evolving holiness. The more you are aware of it and cultivate it, the more quickly you will evolve. A good growing exercise is found in

Quaker prayer services where those gathered are asked, "Let the next sentence out of your mouth come from your highest self." That expression "your highest self" is intriguing—it implies that within each of us are several selves. Consider thinking of them as a trinity of selves: a highest self, a medium or an average self, and a lowest—even primitive—self.

Our highest self is the Spirit-inspired self who possesses unlimited potential for goodness. When this highest self speaks, it does so with love, humility, and compassionate consideration of others' needs before its own. The medium or mediocre self responds like a typical person. It usually makes top priority of its own needs of the moment, is significantly influenced by society's discriminations and prejudices, and strives only to be good, not to become holy. The third or lowest self is the infantile, immaturely selfish self: grudge carrying, suspicious of others, easily aroused to violent and angry outbursts, and often unapologetically prejudiced of other races and the poor. How we respond to any situation depends on which one of those three inner selves we ask to act or speak for us. The law of evolution requires that as often as it is possible, only our highest, most evolved, and mature self speaks or acts. Whenever our highest self speaks and acts, it generates joy as the sun does light.

forty

the oil of **gladness**

Often in the past, our ancestors in faith were told that one day they would reap the rewards of living in joy—in Heaven! But for the time being they had to patiently endure the sufferings of injustice and oppression, the ravages of long hours of inhuman labor, and life's difficult hardships because of Eden's sin. Today, the poor and oppressed are urged to offer passionate, nonviolent resistance to their immoral oppression by the wealthy and powerful. They are not so often asked to wait until the next life to know justice and its companion, joy.

However, the future joy of heavenly bliss continues to be used by funeral preachers to comfort the mourners. At funerals they speak of how the deceased, after the painful trials of this life, is now finally at peace, enjoying the endless happiness of heaven. Death in this theology of deferred joy is imaged as a miraculous revolving door that automatically turns around a person's life of sadness into one of gladness; a life of constant complaining instantly into one of eternal contented bliss. Is this a valid image of the reality that follows death, or does death only solidify—make permanent for all eternity—who you have been in this life?

The Master spoke intensively of the urgent need to always be on your guard so as not to be caught sleeping when death comes to steal your life. Most interesting was his image of death as a bridegroom's unexpected arrival. He surprises the ten waiting bridesmaids who must greet him with their lamps burning brightly. Over the centuries there have been numerous interpretations of this parable of the five foolish wedding attendants whose lamps had used up all their oil.[1] The very multiplicity of interpretations indicates that this is a well-crafted parable, since a good parable should have many levels of meaning. As this book comes to a conclusion, I would like to use this wedding feast parable as an example of the call to be always joyful.

Those who first heard this story would have surely considered the numerous things that oil signified in their culture: healing, the welcoming ritual of a guest, anointing prophets and kings. In Psalm 133, the joy of those harmoniously living together is compared to abundantly flowing oil.

How good it is, how pleasant [joyful]
when people dwell as one!
Like the precious oil on the head,
running down upon the beard.

Oil also had a special Messianic symbolism as "the oil of gladness" was among the Messianic gifts in the prophecy of Second Isaiah. Jesus, the village craftsman, announced the arrival of God's reign in his own hometown by quoting that prophecy, "The spirit of the Lord God is upon me, because the LORD has anointed me." He continued quoting that prophecy, which spoke of bringing glad tidings to the poor, healing the brokenhearted, and releasing prisoners. However, the gospel author of Luke, when reporting those words of Jesus, stops two lines short of Isaiah's very significant Messianic prediction that when the Awaited One came he would:

Provide for those in Zion—
to give them a garland instead of ashes;
the *oil of joy* instead of mourning.[2]

With this concept of the oil of joyfulness, we return to the wedding parable. When the arrival of the bridegroom was announced, the five imprudent attendants found their lamps were out of oil. They were unable to borrow any oil from the other five, who had prudently ensured that their oil supply was kept plentiful. This forced the foolish attendants to go to an oil merchant and buy their needed oil. The Master concludes his parable by saying that while they were off buying oil the bridegroom came, and those whose lamps were burning brightly went into the wedding feast with him. When the other five finally hurried back, they found the door closed and bolted. Standing outside, they pleaded to be admitted, but the bridegroom answered, "Away with you! I don't know who you are!"

The cultural and scriptural symbolism of oil as a sign of joyful gladness was surely known to both the parable teller and his audience. In his teaching Jesus made a point of not explaining his parables, but the writer of Matthew's gospel decided to reinforce the meanings of the parable, having Jesus say, "therefore, keep awake, for you know neither the day nor the hour." He could just as easily have said, "Rejoice always, keep your lives abundant with the oil of gladness, for you know neither the day or the hour of your death. What you lack at your death you can't beg, purchase, or acquire, even by pleading with the Lord!" Does death reward or punish whatever life you're living, or does how you live only confirm your eternal state of existence? Regardless, don't be foolish like those bridesmaids, since the best way to be ready to die is to live joyfully—always!

The Master frequently compared the age of God to a wedding feast, which for the peasant villagers of Palestine was the most jubilant of all their celebrations. The admonition of Thessalonians, "Be always joyful," means being jubilant not simply for a week but to live continuously joyful. If you believe the Master's teaching that the Kingdom of God has arrived, then should you not go about your daily life like a perpetual bridesmaid or groomsman of the wedding feast of that Great Jubilee? In Luke's gospel, Jesus summarizes his destiny by identifying himself as the enfleshment of the jubilee year as Isaiah had prophesied.

> The Spirit of the Lord is upon me,
> because he has anointed me
> to bring good news to the poor.
> He has sent me to proclaim release to the captives
> and recovery of sight to the blind,
> to let the oppressed go free.[3]

In these words is found the oil of joyfulness that ensures that you can be a faithful wedding attendant.

That oil of happiness is a byproduct of living as a faithful resident in the kingdom of Heaven and as a disciple of the Master of the Jubilee. Your heart-lamp is filled to overflowing with the oil of happiness whenever you reach out to assist others, since you become so immersed in what you are doing that you forget yourself. As a good disciple who imitates the Master, you open the eyes of those blinded by routine to the beauties of the ordinary by your joyful pleasure in the commonplace. Simply by your presence as a free person you offer the hope of escape to those too easily held captive by fear of those in authority. Likewise, simply by your happy presence you wordlessly offer the hope of escape to those oppressed by worries and depression. Oil of gladness is also found in caring for the poor, offering a helping hand to anyone in need, and clothing those naked of honor by treating them as important. Paradoxically, the oil of joy bubbles up out of thin air whenever you stop waiting for the Bridegroom to appear and begin rejoicing in celebrating the wedding feast of the Kingdom of God.

Yobhel is Hebrew for "Jubilee." In Latin, this became *Jubilare*, "to raise a shout of joy." Shouting for joy was a spontaneous response for the oppressed, since a jubilee year signaled freedom for slaves and prisoners and, for the oppressed, the canceling of their debts and mortgages. The heart of the Master's message was that the Reign of God had arrived! Not only had this long-awaited age arrived, he and his community were the living incarnations of this new era of an unending jubilee of liberation and joy. "To rejoice always" means striving to live each day being jubilant, regardless of the difficult circumstances, since as a disciple you are a Jubilarian—one who lives in Jubilee time. "By this," the Master could have said, "will all know that you are my disciples, that you are happy, jubilant." Today, everyday, is Jubilee time!

As this book concludes, hear in your heart that dynamic evolutionary message of the Spirit to live joyfully. That message has echoed globally across the millennia in the teachings of spiritual masters, especially Jesus and Paul, "to always rejoice." It echoes in Buddha's words, "Live in joy," and reverberates in the wisdom of the Jewish Hasidic masters who say it again: "Live in joy!"

[1] Matthew 25:1–13
[2] Isaiah 61:1–3
[3] Luke 4:18

A s rich benefactors of the American Revolution, we strive to always defend our various rights as set forth in the Declaration of Independence which declares that we are endowed by our Creator with certain inalienable rights, among which are life, liberty, and the pursuit of happiness. As we have reflected in these pages, this quest to live a joyful life is, for personal, social, and political reasons, a truly heroic challenge. Aware of that reality, this book could be seen as a survival manual for striving to live joyously regardless of how dismal or depressing your circumstances. It can also be viewed as a guidebook for the adventuresome pursuit in a bittersweet world of your God-given right and call to happiness. Living in joy is a human freedom the Creator endowed, not just to the people of one nation, but to all the world's peoples.

During the Second World War, Austrian psychiatrist Viktor Frankl was interned in a Nazi concentration camp. As a despised Jewish prisoner he had to endure atrocious and the most degrading of conditions, yet Frankl remained inwardly a free man because he *chose* to be! After his release he would say in *Man's Search for Meaning*, "The last of the human freedoms: to choose one's attitude in any given circumstance, to choose one's own way." This human freedom of choice is an unspoken one included among the others in the Declaration of Independence. It is freedom that no government, religion, or any other group—no matter how powerful—can ever take from you.

To live joyfully in any given circumstance, regardless how horrible it might be, requires making a primary life choice. We have the freedom to choose always being a joyful person and to support this choice by also striving to be always prayerful and grateful. It is absolutely essential that this choice be made as a personal decision, since happiness cannot be left to chance or occasional strokes of good fortune.

May this small book, then, inspire you to make that primal life choice, to dedicate yourself to tirelessly pursuing a life of joy and happiness, a joy that no one can take away from you.

EDWARD HAYS, a Catholic priest of the Archdiocese of Kansas City, is the cofounder of and a moving spirit behind Forest of Peace Publishing. He is the author of more than thirty best-selling books on contemporary spirituality. Many bear his own art. He has also served as director of Shantivanam, a Midwest center for contemplative prayer, and as a chaplain at the state penitentiary in Lansing, Kansas. He has spent extended periods of pilgrimage in the Near East, the Holy Land, and India. He continues his ministry as a prolific writer and painter while remaining active as a spiritual director in Leavenworth, Kansas.

More from Ed Hays

Pray All Ways
A Book for Daily Worship Using All Your Senses
Featuring a new introduction and beautifully designed text for reflective reading and prayer, *Pray All Ways* stresses God's gift of our senses. Readers learn how to pray with their eyes and noses, taste buds and hunger pains, hands and feet. Each of the fifteen chapters features ways to pray as well as the author's original, creative, and soul-stirring prayers. Hays invites readers—whether they are on the go or at rest, awake or asleep—to celebrate the Creator by enjoying and sharing God's gift of prayer.
ISBN: 9780939516810 / 224 pages / $12.95

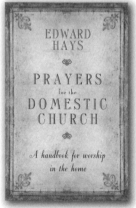

Twenty-Fifth Anniversary Edition
Prayers for the Domestic Church
A Handbook for Worship in the Home
This new edition with a new foreword by the author celebrates the "domestic church"—a family worshipping together at home—with a collection of prayers and blessings that remain as fresh and creative today as they were over twenty-five years ago. With blessings for birthdays, family members, the home, pets, and more, this book makes it easy and fun to gather in prayer as a family. This book is an ideal gift for weddings, baptisms, the birth of a child, special family milestones, and sacred moments.
ISBN: 9780939516797 / 288 pages / $17.95

Available from your bookstore or from
ave maria press / Notre Dame, IN 46556
www.avemariapress.com / Ph: 800-282-1865
A Ministry of the Indiana Province of Holy Cross